Consulate Processing Application for the DS-260

Getting the Green Card Overseas from a Spouse

Attorney Brian D. Lerner

LAW OFFICES OF BRIAN D. LERNER A PROFESSIONAL CORPORATION

ATTORNEY DRAFTED IMMIGRATION PETITIONS

By

Brian D. Lerner

Attorney at Law

Disclaimer and Terms of Use:

Effort has been made to ensure that the information in this book is accurate and complete. However, the author and the publisher do not warrant that this particular petition will mirror or be exactly as your situation. There has not been any attorney-client agreement created by the purchase of this petition or application. No legal advice has occurred. The cases, regulations and/or statutes cited may change at any time without notice.

ISBN: 978-1-958990-44-5

INTRODUCTION

There are a multitude of different immigration petitions and applications. They are complex and full of requirements. Obviously, it would be best to hire an immigration attorney to best prepare the petitions and applications. However, this can certainly cost thousands of dollars.

The next best option is to get a sample of the petition written by an experienced immigration attorney. The samples cost a fraction what would be charged by an immigration attorney. However, while the reader has to alter, amend and change the parts of the sample petition to reflect their actual situation, it is a fantastic roadmap for them to use. If the reader has purchased the entire petition or application, they will have real live samples of cover letters, forms, declarations, affidavits and the necessary exhibits to use. The samples come from real cases and the names of those clients have been redacted to protect the privacy of that person or corporation.

These are petitions and applications that have been drafted by an experienced immigration attorney with over 25 years of experience. Get the benefits of that experience without the costs.

CONTENTS

About the Law Offices of Brian D. Lerner

The Law Offices of Brian D. Lerner, APC. The law practice consists of Immigration and Nationality Law and everything involved with and regarding immigration which includes citizenship, investment visas, family and employment visas, removal and deportation hearings, appeals, waivers, adjustment, consulate processing and all types of immigration and citizenship matters. Thousands of families have been reunited and/or permitted to stay in the U.S. and/or return to the U.S. because of the successful work of Immigration Attorney Brian D. Lerner.

This law offices handles all types of immigration cases including family based and employment based. Immigration issues range from immigration court proceedings to trying to fix what paralegals may have done that was neither correct nor proper. Foreign nationals must have experience lawyers admitted to practice law.

The Law Offices of Brian D. Lerner, APC, handles cases arising from business visas, work permits, Green Cards, non-immigrant visas, deportation, citizenship, appeals and all areas of immigration. The Law Offices of Brian D. Lerner, APC does EB-5 Investor Visas, H-1B Specialty Occupation, L-1 Intracompany Transferee, E-2 Treaty Investor, E-1 Treaty Trader, O-1 Extraordinary Ability among others. Regarding immigrant visas for the Green Card, the firm does PERM and advanced degree PERM, Family Petitions, and Extraordinary Alien Petitions. In addition to affirmative petitions, the Law Firm represents people in people in deportation and removal hearings, including political asylum, withholding of removal, and convention against torture cases.

Brian D. Lerner has been certified as an expert in Immigration & Nationality Law by the California State Bar, Board of Legal Specialization since 2000 and has been re-certified three times. He now passes on his decades of experience by allowing the Reader, Law Schools, Professors and other Immigration Attorneys to purchase sample petitions on every facet of Immigration Law.

About the Consulate Processing Application

Married to a U.S. Citizen or Lawful Permanent Resident and want to now come to the U.S. as a Lawful Permanent Resident? You miss your spouse and want to be together, but do not know what to do or how to do it? This Consulate Processing package or 'Spousal Visa Petition' is what you will need. If approved, then you could be here in the U.S. in under a year. However, as many of you know, if not done properly, you could get a denial and be stuck in your home country for years. Remember, it is your responsibility to submit everything correctly. This sample Consulate Processing Spousal Visa Petition has everything necessary to give you the best chance possible to get an approval. Just input your own information and use the application as a guide. It has been prepared by an expert Immigration Attorney. Thus, this book will allow you to see a guide of how it is done, prepared and submitted.

ATTORNEY COVER LETTER

Law Offices of Brian D. Lerner

A PROFESSIONAL CORPORATION

CERTIFIED SPECIALIST IN IMMIGRATION AND NATIONALITY LAW
ADMITTED TO THE U.S. SUPREME COURT

LONG BEACH, CALIFORNIA
(562) 495-0554
CARSON, CALIFORNIA
(310) 684-5410

October 16, 2017

National Visa Center
Attn: CMR
31 Rochester Avenue, Suite 100
Portsmouth, NH 03801-2914

Re: Application for U.S. Immigrant Visa
Petitioner: [redacted]
Applicant: [redacted]
NVC Case Number: CDJ2016801007

Dear Sir/Madam:

We hereby submit the following in support of [redacted] (hereinafter as "Applicant") Immigrant Visa application. The required Immigrant Visa Fee and Affidavit of Support Fee have been paid electronically (see **Exhibit '7'**). The DS-260, Immigrant Visa Electronic Application, has also been submitted electronically (see **Exhibit '8'**).

Enclosed herein please find the following documents:

FORMS

FORMS:	**DESCRIPTION:**
G-28	Notice of Entry of Appearance as Attorney or Accredited Representative of the Petitioner;
G-28	Notice of Entry of Appearance as Attorney or Accredited Representative of the Beneficiary;
I-864	Affidavit of Support Under Section 213A of the INA

We also enclose two passport-style photographs of the Petitioner and Beneficiary.

EXHIBITS

EXHIBIT:	**DESCRIPTION:**
'1'	Petitioner's Birth Certificate;
'2'	Petitioner's Passport;
'3'	Applicant's Birth Certificate with English Translation;

'4'	Applicant's Marriage Certificate with English Translation;
'5'	Applicant's Passport;
'6'	Proof of Relationship Between Petitioner and Applicant;
'7'	Proof of Payment of Immigrant Visa Fee;
'8'	Confirmation of DS-260 Immigrant Visa Electronic Application;
'9'	Correction Sheet of DS-260 Immigrant Visa Electronic Application;
'10'	I-130 Approval Notice of Applicant and Petitioner; and
'11'	Petitioner's 2016 Tax Return with W-2 Form.

Based on the foregoing, we believe that the NVC has everything necessary to forward Applicant's case to the U.S. Consulate for final processing. Thank you for your consideration in this matter.

Should you have any further questions, please feel free to contact our office at (562) 495-0554.

Sincerely,

Brian D. Lerner
Attorney at Law

FORMS

Notice of Entry of Appearance as Attorney or Accredited Representative

Department of Homeland Security

DHS Form G-28
OMB No. 1615-0105
Expires 03/31/2018

Part 1. Information About Attorney or Accredited Representative

1. USCIS ELIS Account Number *(if any)* ▶

Name and Address of Attorney or Accredited Representative

2.a. Family Name *(Last Name)* Lerner

2.b. Given Name *(First Name)* Brian

2.c. Middle Name D

3.a. Street Number and Name 3233 E Broadway

3.b. Apt. ☐ Ste. ☐ Flr. ☐

3.c. City or Town Long Beach

3.d. State CA 3.e. ZIP Code 90803

3.f. Province

3.g. Postal Code

3.h. Country USA

4. Daytime Telephone Number 5624950554

5. Fax Number 5626088672

6. E-Mail Address *(if any)* blerner@californiaimmigration.us

7. Mobile Telephone Number *(if any)*

Part 2. Notice of Appearance as Attorney or Accredited Representative

This appearance relates to immigration matters before *(Select only one box)*:

1.a. ☒ USCIS

1.b. List the form numbers I-864

2.a. ☐ ICE

2.b. List the specific matter in which appearance is entered

3.a. ☐ CBP

3.b. List the specific matter in which appearance is entered

I enter my appearance as attorney or accredited representative at the request of:

4. Select only one box:
☐ Applicant ☒ Petitioner ☐ Requestor
☐ Respondent (ICE, CBP)

Information About Applicant, Petitioner, Requestor, or Respondent

5.a. Family Name *(Last Name)* [redacted]

5.b. Given Name *(First Name)* [redacted]

5.c. Middle Name [redacted]

6. Name of Company or Organization *(if applicable)*

Part 2. Notice of Appearance as Attorney or Accredited Representative *(continued)*

Information About Applicant, Petitioner, Requestor, or Respondent (continued)

7. USCIS ELIS Account Number *(if any)*

▶

8. Alien Registration Number (A-Number) or Receipt Number

9. Daytime Telephone Number

10. Mobile Telephone Number *(if any)*

11. E-Mail Address *(if any)*

yahoo.com

Mailing Address of Applicant, Petitioner, Requestor, or Respondent

NOTE: Provide the mailing address of the applicant, petitioner, requestor, or respondent. **Do not** provide the business mailing address of the attorney or accredited representative **unless** it serves as the safe mailing address on the application, petition, or request being filed with this Form G-28.

12.a. Street Number and Name

12.b. Apt. ☐ Ste. ☐ Flr. ☐

12.c. City or Town: Honolulu

12.d. State: HI 12.e. ZIP Code: 96819

12.f. Province

12.g. Postal Code

12.h. Country: USA

Part 3. Eligibility Information for Attorney or Accredited Representative

Select **all applicable** items.

1.a. ☒ I am an attorney eligible to practice law in, and a member in good standing of, the bar of the highest courts of the following states, possessions, territories, commonwealths, or the District of Columbia. *(If you need additional space, use **Part 6.**)*

Licensing Authority: Supreme Court of California

1.b. Bar Number *(if applicable)*: 158536

1.c. Name of Law Firm: Law Offices of Brian D. Lerner

1.d. I *(choose one)* ☒ ***am not*** ☐ ***am***

subject to any order of any court or administrative agency disbarring, suspending, enjoining, restraining, or otherwise restricting me in the practice of law. If you are subject to any orders, explain in the space below. *(If you need additional space, use **Part 6.**)*

2.a. ☐ I am an accredited representative of the following qualified nonprofit religious, charitable, social service, or similar organization established in the United States, so recognized by the Department of Justice, Board of Immigration Appeals, in accordance with 8 CFR 292.2. Provide the name of the organization and the expiration date of accreditation.

2.b. Name of Recognized Organization

2.c. Date accreditation expires *(mm/dd/yyyy)* ▶

Part 3. Eligibility Information for Attorney or Accredited Representative *(continued)*

3. ☐ I am associated with [ ], the attorney or accredited representative of record who previously filed Form G-28 in this case, and my appearance as an attorney or accredited representative is at his or her request.

   NOTE: If you select this item, also complete **Item Numbers 1.a. - 1.b. or Item Numbers 2.a. - 2.c.** in **Part 3.** *(whichever is appropriate)*.

4.a. ☐ I am a law student or law graduate working under the direct supervision of the attorney or accredited representative of record on this form in accordance with the requirements in 8 CFR 292.1(a)(2)(iv).

4.b. Name of Law Student or Law Graduate [ ]

Part 4. Applicant, Petitioner, Requestor, or Respondent Consent to Representation, Contact Information, and Signature

Consent to Representation and Release of Information

1. I have requested the representation of and consented to being represented by the attorney or accredited representative named in **Part 1.** of this form. According to the Privacy Act of 1974 and DHS policy, I also consent to the disclosure to the named attorney or accredited representative of any record pertaining to me that appears in any system of records of USCIS, ICE or CBP.

   When you (the applicant, petitioner, requestor, or respondent) are represented, DHS will send notices to both you and your attorney or accredited representative either through mail or electronic delivery.

   DHS will also send the Form I-94, Arrival Departure Record, to you **unless** you select **Item Number 2.a.** in **Part 4.** All secure identity documents and Travel Documents will be sent to you (the applicant, petitioner, requestor, or respondent) at your U.S. mailing address **unless** you ask us to send your secure identity documents to your attorney of record or accredited representative.

   If you do not want to receive original notices or secure identity documents directly, but would rather have such notices and documents sent to your attorney of record or accredited representative, please select **all applicable** boxes below:

2.a ☒ I request DHS send any notice (including Form I-94) on an application, petition, or request to the U.S. business address of my attorney of record or accredited representative as listed in this form. I understand that I may change this election at any future date through written notice to DHS.

2.b. ☐ I request that DHS send any secure identity document, such as a Permanent Resident Card, Employment Authorization Document, or Travel Document, that I am approved to receive and authorized to possess, to the U.S. business address of my attorney of record or accredited representative as listed in this form or to a designated military or diplomatic address for pickup in a foreign country (if permitted). I consent to having my secure identity document sent to my attorney of record or accredited representative's U.S. business address and understand that I may request, at any future date and through written notice to DHS, that DHS send any secure identity document to me directly.

3.a. Signature of Applicant, Petitioner, Requestor, or Respondent

➡ [redacted]

3.b. Date of Signature *(mm/dd/yyyy)*▶ 10/1/17

Part 5. Signature of Attorney or Accredited Representative

I have read and understand the regulations and conditions contained in 8 CFR 103.2 and 292 governing appearances and representation before the Department of Homeland Security. I declare under penalty of perjury under the laws of the United States that the information I have provided on this form is true and correct.

1. Signature of Attorney or Accredited Representative [signature]

2. Signature of Law Student or Law Graduate [ ]

3. Date of Signature *(mm/dd/yyyy)*▶ [ ]

Part 6. Additional Information

Use the space provided below to provide additional information pertaining to **Part 3., Item Numbers 1.a. - 1.d.** or to provide your U.S. business address for purposes of receiving secure identity documents for your client (if your client has consented to your receipt of such documents under **Part 4.**)

Notice of Entry of Appearance as Attorney or Accredited Representative

Department of Homeland Security

DHS Form G-28
OMB No. 1615-0105
Expires 03/31/2018

Part 1. Information About Attorney or Accredited Representative

1. USCIS ELIS Account Number *(if any)*

Name and Address of Attorney or Accredited Representative

2.a. Family Name *(Last Name)* Lerner
2.b. Given Name *(First Name)* Brian
2.c. Middle Name D
3.a. Street Number and Name 3233 E Broadway
3.b. Apt. ☐ Ste. ☐ Flr. ☐
3.c. City or Town Long Beach
3.d. State CA 3.e. ZIP Code 90803
3.f. Province
3.g. Postal Code
3.h. Country USA
4. Daytime Telephone Number 5624950554
5. Fax Number 5626088672
6. E-Mail Address *(if any)* blerner@californiaimmigration.us
7. Mobile Telephone Number *(if any)*

Part 2. Notice of Appearance as Attorney or Accredited Representative

This appearance relates to immigration matters before *(Select only one box)*:

1.a. ☒ USCIS
1.b. List the form numbers I-864
2.a. ☐ ICE
2.b. List the specific matter in which appearance is entered
3.a. ☐ CBP
3.b. List the specific matter in which appearance is entered

I enter my appearance as attorney or accredited representative at the request of:

4. **Select only one box:**
☒ Applicant ☐ Petitioner ☐ Requestor
☐ Respondent (ICE, CBP)

Information About Applicant, Petitioner, Requestor, or Respondent

5.a. Family Name *(Last Name)* [redacted]
5.b. Given Name *(First Name)* [redacted]
5.c. Middle Name
6. Name of Company or Organization *(if applicable)*

Part 2. Notice of Appearance as Attorney or Accredited Representative *(continued)*

Information About Applicant, Petitioner, Requestor, or Respondent (continued)

7. USCIS ELIS Account Number *(if any)*

▶

8. Alien Registration Number (A-Number) or Receipt Number

9. Daytime Telephone Number

10. Mobile Telephone Number *(if any)*

11. E-Mail Address *(if any)*

rol d ahoo.com

Mailing Address of Applicant, Petitioner, Requestor, or Respondent

NOTE: Provide the mailing address of the applicant, petitioner, requestor, or respondent. **Do not** provide the business mailing address of the attorney or accredited representative **unless** it serves as the safe mailing address on the application, petition, or request being filed with this Form G-28.

12.a. Street Number and Name

12.b. Apt. ☐ Ste. ☐ Flr. ☐

12.c. City or Town

12.d. State

12.e. ZIP Code

12.f. Province Hidalgo

12.g. Postal Code 43600

12.h. Country

Mexico

Part 3. Eligibility Information for Attorney or Accredited Representative

Select **all applicable** items.

1.a. ☒ I am an attorney eligible to practice law in, and a member in good standing of, the bar of the highest courts of the following states, possessions, territories, commonwealths, or the District of Columbia. *(If you need additional space, use Part 6.)*

Licensing Authority

Supreme Court of California

1.b. Bar Number *(if applicable)*

158536

1.c. Name of Law Firm

Law Offices of Brian D. Lerner

1.d. I *(choose one)* ☒ ***am not*** ☐ ***am***

subject to any order of any court or administrative agency disbarring, suspending, enjoining, restraining, or otherwise restricting me in the practice of law. If you are subject to any orders, explain in the space below. *(If you need additional space, use Part 6.)*

2.a. ☐ I am an accredited representative of the following qualified nonprofit religious, charitable, social service, or similar organization established in the United States, so recognized by the Department of Justice, Board of Immigration Appeals, in accordance with 8 CFR 292.2. Provide the name of the organization and the expiration date of accreditation.

2.b. Name of Recognized Organization

2.c. Date accreditation expires

(mm/dd/yyyy) ▶

Part 3. Eligibility Information for Attorney or Accredited Representative *(continued)*

3. ☐ I am associated with

[ ],

the attorney or accredited representative of record who previously filed Form G-28 in this case, and my appearance as an attorney or accredited representative is at his or her request.

NOTE: If you select this item, also complete **Item Numbers 1.a. - 1.b. or Item Numbers 2.a. - 2.c.** in **Part 3.** *(whichever is appropriate).*

4.a. ☐ I am a law student or law graduate working under the direct supervision of the attorney or accredited representative of record on this form in accordance with the requirements in 8 CFR 292.1(a)(2)(iv).

4.b. Name of Law Student or Law Graduate

[ ]

Part 4. Applicant, Petitioner, Requestor, or Respondent Consent to Representation, Contact Information, and Signature

Consent to Representation and Release of Information

1. I have requested the representation of and consented to being represented by the attorney or accredited representative named in **Part 1.** of this form. According to the Privacy Act of 1974 and DHS policy, I also consent to the disclosure to the named attorney or accredited representative of any record pertaining to me that appears in any system of records of USCIS, ICE or CBP.

When you (the applicant, petitioner, requestor, or respondent) are represented, DHS will send notices to both you and your attorney or accredited representative either through mail or electronic delivery.

DHS will also send the Form I-94, Arrival Departure Record, to you **unless** you select **Item Number 2.a.** in **Part 4.** All secure identity documents and Travel Documents will be sent to you (the applicant, petitioner, requestor, or respondent) at your U.S. mailing address **unless** you ask us to send your secure identity documents to your attorney of record or accredited representative.

If you do not want to receive original notices or secure identity documents directly, but would rather have such notices and documents sent to your attorney of record or accredited representative, please select **all applicable** boxes below:

2.a ☒ I request DHS send any notice (including Form I-94) on an application, petition, or request to the U.S. business address of my attorney of record or accredited representative as listed in this form. I understand that I may change this election at any future date through written notice to DHS.

2.b. ☐ I request that DHS send any secure identity document, such as a Permanent Resident Card, Employment Authorization Document, or Travel Document, that I am approved to receive and authorized to possess, to the U.S. business address of my attorney of record or accredited representative as listed in this form or to a designated military or diplomatic address for pickup in a foreign country (if permitted). I consent to having my secure identity document sent to my attorney of record or accredited representative's U.S. business address and understand that I may request, at any future date and through written notice to DHS, that DHS send any secure identity document to me directly.

3.a. Signature of Applicant, Petitioner, Requestor, or Respondent

➡ [signature]

3.b. Date of Signature *(mm/dd/yyyy)* ▶ 10-1-23

Part 5. Signature of Attorney or Accredited Representative

I have read and understand the regulations and conditions contained in 8 CFR 103.2 and 292 governing appearances and representation before the Department of Homeland Security. I declare under penalty of perjury under the laws of the United States that the information I have provided on this form is true and correct.

1. Signature of Attorney or Accredited Representative

[signature]

2. Signature of Law Student or Law Graduate

[ ]

3. Date of Signature *(mm/dd/yyyy)* ▶ [ ]

Part 6. Additional Information

Use the space provided below to provide additional information pertaining to **Part 3., Item Numbers 1.a. - 1.d.** or to provide your U.S. business address for purposes of receiving secure identity documents for your client (if your client has consented to your receipt of such documents under **Part 4.**)

Current Mailing Address:

MEXICO 43600

Affidavit of Support Under Section 213A of the INA

Department of Homeland Security
U.S. Citizenship and Immigration Services

USCIS
Form I-864
OMB No. 1615-0075
Expires 07/31/2017

For USCIS Use Only	Affidavit of Support Submitter	Section 213A Review	Number of Support Affidavits in File
	☐ Petitioner ☐ 1st Joint Sponsor ☐ 2nd Joint Sponsor ☐ Substitute Sponsor ☐ 5% Owner	☐ MEETS requirements ☐ DOES NOT MEET requirements Reviewed By:________ Office:________ Date (mm/dd/yyyy):________	☐ 1 ☐ 2 **Remarks**

▶ **START HERE - Type or print in black ink.**

Part 1. Basis For Filing Affidavit of Support

I, [redacted] a[...]vit of support because (Select only one box):

1.a. ☒ I am the petitioner. I filed or am filing for the immigration of my relative.

1.b. ☐ I filed an alien worker petition on behalf of the intending immigrant, who is related to me as my

1.c. ☐ I have an ownership interest of at least 5 percent in

which filed an alien worker petition on behalf of the intending immigrant, who is related to me as my

1.d. ☐ I am the only joint sponsor.

1.e. ☐ I am the ☐ first ☐ second of two joint sponsors.

1.f. ☐ The original petitioner is deceased. I am the substitute sponsor. I am the intending immigrant's

NOTE: If you select Item Number 1.a., 1.b., 1.c., 1.d., 1.e., or 1.f., you must include proof of your U.S. citizenship, U.S. national status, or lawful permanent resident status.

Part 2. Information About the Principal Immigrant

1.a. Family Name (Last Name) [redacted]

1.b. Given Name (First Name) [redacted]

1.c. Middle Name

Mailing Address

2.a. In Care Of Name

2.b. Street Number and Name [redacted]

2.c. ☐ Apt. ☐ Ste. ☐ Flr.

2.d. City or Town [redacted]

2.e. State **2.f.** ZIP Code

2.g. Province Hidalgo

2.h. Postal Code 43600

2.i. Country Mexico

Part 2. Information About the Principal Immigrant (continued)

Other Information

3. Country of Citizenship or Nationality
Mexico

4. Date of Birth (mm/dd/yyyy) 02/24/1980

5. Alien Registration Number (A-Number) (if any)
► A-

6. USCIS ELIS Account Number (if any)
►

7. Daytime Telephone Number

Part 3. Information About the Immigrants You Are Sponsoring

1. I am sponsoring the principal immigrant named in **Part 2.**
☒ Yes ☐ No (Applicable only if you are sponsoring family members in **Part 3.** as the second joint sponsor)

2. ☐ I am sponsoring the following family members immigrating at the same time or within six months of the principal immigrant named in **Part 2.** (Do not include any relative listed on a separate visa petition.)

Family Member 1

3.a. Family Name (Last Name)

3.b. Given Name (First Name)

3.c. Middle Name

4. Relationship to Sponsored Immigrant

5. Date of Birth (mm/dd/yyyy)

6. Alien Registration Number (A-Number) (if any)
► A-

7. USCIS ELIS Account Number (if any)
►

Family Member 2

8.a. Family Name (Last Name)

8.b. Given Name (First Name)

8.c. Middle Name

9. Relationship to Sponsored Immigrant

10. Date of Birth (mm/dd/yyyy)

11. Alien Registration Number (A-Number) (if any)
► A-

12. USCIS ELIS Account Number (if any)
►

Family Member 3

13.a. Family Name (Last Name)

13.b. Given Name (First Name)

13.c. Middle Name

14. Relationship to Sponsored Immigrant

15. Date of Birth (mm/dd/yyyy)

16. Alien Registration Number (A-Number) (if any)
► A-

17. USCIS ELIS Account Number (if any)
►

Family Member 4

18.a. Family Name (Last Name)

18.b. Given Name (First Name)

18.c. Middle Name

Part 3. Information About the Immigrants You Are Sponsoring (continued)

19. Relationship to Sponsored Immigrant

20. Date of Birth (mm/dd/yyyy)

21. Alien Registration Number (A-Number) (if any) ► A-

22. USCIS ELIS Account Number (if any) ►

Family Member 5

23.a. Family Name (Last Name)

23.b. Given Name (First Name)

23.c. Middle Name

24. Relationship to Sponsored Immigrant

25. Date of Birth (mm/dd/yyyy)

26. Alien Registration Number (A-Number) (if any) ► A-

27. USCIS ELIS Account Number (if any) ►

28. Enter the total number of immigrants you are sponsoring on this affidavit from **Item Numbers 1.a. - 27.** 1

Part 4. Information About You (Sponsor)

Sponsor's Full Name

1.a. Family Name (Last Name)

1.b. Given Name (First Name)

1.c. Middle Name

Sponsor's Mailing Address

2.a. In Care Of Name

2.b. Street Number and Name

2.c. ☐ Apt. ☐ Ste. ☐ Flr.

2.d. City or Town Honolulu

2.e. State HI 2.f. ZIP Code 96819

2.g. Province

2.h. Postal Code

2.i. Country USA

3. Is your current mailing address the same as your physical address? ☒ Yes ☐ No

If you answered "No" to **Item Number 3.**, provide your physical address below.

Sponsor's Physical Address

4.a. Street Number and Name

4.b. ☐ Apt. ☐ Ste. ☐ Flr.

4.c. City or Town

4.d. State 4.e. ZIP Code

4.f. Province

4.g. Postal Code

4.h. Country

For USCIS Use Only	

Part 4. Information About You (Sponsor) (continued)

Other Information

5. Country of Domicile: USA

6. Date of Birth (mm/dd/yyyy): 01/22/1976

7. City or Town of Birth: Honolulu

8. State or Province of Birth: Hawaii

9. Country of Birth: USA

10. U.S. Social Security Number (Required) ► [redacted]

Citizenship or Residency

11.a. [X] I am a U.S. citizen.

11.b. [ ] I am a U.S. national.

11.c. [ ] I am a lawful permanent resident.

12. Sponsor's A-Number (if any) ► A-

13. Sponsor's USCIS ELIS Account Number (if any) ►

Military Service (To be completed by petitioner sponsors only.)

14. I am currently on **active duty** in the U.S. Armed Forces or U.S. Coast Guard. [ ] Yes [X] No

Part 5. Sponsor's Household Size

NOTE: Do not count any member of your household more than once.

Persons you are sponsoring in this affidavit:

1. Provide the number you entered in **Part 3., Item Number 28.** 1

Persons NOT sponsored in this affidavit:

2. Yourself. 1

3. If you are currently married, enter "1" for your spouse.

4. If you have dependent children, enter the number here. 2

5. If you have any other dependents, enter the number here.

6. If you have sponsored any other persons on Form I-864 or Form I-864 EZ who are now lawful permanent residents, enter the number here.

7. **OPTIONAL:** If you have siblings, parents, or adult children with the same principal residence who are combining their income with yours by submitting Form I-864A, enter the number here.

8. Add together **Part 5., Item Numbers 1. - 7.** and enter the number here. **Household Size:** 4

For USCIS Use Only	

Part 6. Sponsor's Employment and Income

I am currently:

1.a. [X] Employed as a/an

Financial Service Representative

1.a.1. Name of Employer 1 (if applicable)

Hawaii USA Federal Credit Union

1.a.2. Name of Employer 2 (if applicable)

1.b. [ ] Selfemployed as a/an (Occupation)

1.c. [ ] Retired From (Company Name)

since (mm/dd/yyyy)

1.d. [ ] Unemployed

since (mm/dd/yyyy)

2. My current individual annual income is:

$

Income you are using from any other person who was counted in your household size, including, in certain conditions, the intending immigrant. (See Form I-864 Instructions.) Please indicate name, relationship, and income.

Person 1

3. Name

4. Relationship

5. **Current Income** $

Person 2

6. Name

7. Relationship

8. **Current Income** $

Person 3

9. Name

10. Relationship

11. **Current Income** $

Person 4

12. Name

13. Relationship

14. **Current Income** $

15. **My Current Annual Household Income** (Total all lines from **Part 6., Item Numbers 2., 5., 8., 11.,** and **14.**; the total will be compared to Federal Poverty Guidelines on Form I-864P.)

$

16. [ ] The people listed in **Item Numbers** , **9.**, and **12.** have completed Form I-864A. I am filing along with this affidavit all necessary Form I-864As completed by these people.

For USCIS Use Only	Household Size	Poverty Guideline	Remarks
	☐ 1 ☐ 2 ☐ 3 ☐ 4 ☐ 5 ☐ 6 ☐ 7 ☐ 8 ☐ 9 ☐ Other_____	Year: 20___ Poverty Line: $_____	

Part 6. Sponsor's Employment and Income (continued)

17. ☐ One or more of the people listed in **Item Numbers 3., 6., 9.,** and **12.** do not need to complete Form I-864A because he or she is the intending immigrant and has no accompanying dependents.

Name

Federal Income Tax Return Information

18.a. Have you filed a Federal income tax return for each of the three most recent tax years? ☒ Yes ☐ No

NOTE: You **MUST** attach a photocopy or transcript of your Federal income tax return for only the most recent tax year.

18.b. ☐ (Optional) I have attached photocopies or transcripts of my Federal income tax returns for my second and third most recent tax years.

My total income (adjusted gross income on Internal Revenue Service (IRS) Form 1040EZ) as reported on my Federal income tax returns for the most recent three years was:

	Tax Year	Total Income
19.a. Most Recent	2016	$ 35271
19.b. 2nd Most Recent	2015	$ 31850
19.c. 3rd Most Recent	2014	$ 31850

20. ☐ I was not required to file a Federal income tax return as my income was below the IRS required level and I have attached evidence to support this.

Part 7. Use of Assets to Supplement Income (Optional)

If your income, or the total income for you and your household, from Part 6., Item Numbers 19.a. - 19.c., exceeds the Federal Poverty Guidelines for your household size, YOU ARE NOT REQUIRED to complete this Part 7. Skip to Part 8.

Your Assets (Optional)

1. Enter the balance of all savings and checking accounts. $

2. Enter the net cash value of real-estate holdings. (Net value means current assessed value minus mortgage debt.) $

3. Enter the net cash value of all stocks, bonds, certificates of deposit, and any other assets not already included in **Item Number 1.** or **Item Number 2.** $

4. **Add together Item Numbers 1. - 3. and enter the number here.** **TOTAL:** $

Assets from Form I-864A, Part 4., Item Number 3.d., for:

5.a. Name of Relative

5.b. **Your household member's assets from Form I-864A** (optional). $

Assets of the principal sponsored immigrant (optional). The principal sponsored immigrant is the person listed in **Part 2., Item Numbers 1.a. - 1.c.**

6. Enter the balance of the sponsored immigrant's savings and checking accounts. $

For USCIS Use Only	Household Size	Poverty Guideline	Sponsor's Household Income (Page 5, Line 10)	Remarks
	☐ 1 ☐ 2 ☐ 3 ☐ 4 ☐ 5 ☐ 6 ☐ 7 ☐ 8 ☐ 9 ☐ Other______	Year: 20___	$______	
		Poverty Line: $______	*The total value of all assets, line 10, must equal 5 times (3 times for spouses and children of USC's, or 1 time for orphans to be formally adopted in the U.S.) the difference between the poverty guidelines and the sponsor's household income, line 10.*	

Part 7. Use of Assets to Supplement Income (Optional) (continued)

7. Enter the net cash value of all the sponsored immigrant's real estate holdings. (Net value means investment value minus mortgage debt.) $______

8. Enter the current cash value of the sponsored immigrant's stocks, bonds, certificates of deposit, and other assets not included in **Item Number 6.** or **Item Number 7.** $______

9. **Add together Item Numbers 6. - 8. and enter the number here.** $______

Total Value of Assets

10. **Add together Item Numbers 4., 5.b., and 9. and enter the number here.** TOTAL: $______

Part 8. Sponsor's Contract, Statement, Contact Information, Certification, and Signature

NOTE: Read the information on penalties in the **Penalties** section of the Form I-864 Instructions before completing this part.

Sponsor's Contract

Please note that, by signing this Form I-864, you agree to assume certain specific obligations under the Immigration and Nationality Act (INA) and other Federal laws. The following paragraphs describe those obligations. Please read the following information carefully before you sign Form I-864. If you do not understand the obligations, you may wish to consult an attorney or accredited representative.

What is the Legal Effect of My Signing Form I-864?

If you sign Form I-864 on behalf of any person (called the intending immigrant) who is applying for an immigrant visa or for adjustment of status to a lawful permanent resident, and that intending immigrant submits Form I-864 to the U.S. Government with his or her application for an immigrant visa or adjustment of status, under INA section 213A, these actions create a contract between you and the U.S. Government. The intending immigrant becoming a lawful permanent resident is the consideration for the contract.

Under this contract, you agree that, in deciding whether the intending immigrant can establish that he or she is not inadmissible to the United States as a person likely to become a public charge, the U.S. Government can consider your income and assets as available for the support of the intending immigrant.

What If I Choose Not to Sign Form I-864?

The U.S. Government cannot make you sign Form I-864 if you do not want to do so. But if you do not sign Form I-864, the intending immigrant may not become a lawful permanent resident in the United States.

What Does Signing Form I-864 Require Me to do?

If an intending immigrant becomes a lawful permanent resident in the United States based on a Form I-864 that you have signed, then, until your obligations under Form I-864 terminate, you must:

A. Provide the intending immigrant any support necessary to maintain him or her at an income that is at least 125 percent of the Federal Poverty Guidelines for his or her household size (100 percent if you are the petitioning sponsor and are on active duty in the U.S. Armed Forces or U.S. Coast Guard, and the person is your husband, wife, or unmarried child under 21 years of age); and

Part 8. Sponsor's Contract, Statement, Contact Information, Certification, and Signature (continued)

B. Notify U.S. Citizenship and Immigration Services (USCIS) of any change in your address, within 30 days of the change, by filing Form I-865.

What Other Consequences Are There?

If an intending immigrant becomes a lawful permanent resident in the United States based on a Form I-864 that you have signed, then, until your obligations under Form I-864 terminate, the U.S. Government may consider (deem) your income and assets as available to that person, in determining whether he or she is eligible for certain Federal means-tested public benefits and also for state or local means-tested public benefits, if the state or local government's rules provide for consideration (deeming) of your income and assets as available to the person.

This provision does **not** apply to public benefits specified in section 403(c) of the Welfare Reform Act such as emergency Medicaid, short-term, non-cash emergency relief; services provided under the National School Lunch and Child Nutrition Acts; immunizations and testing and treatment for communicable diseases; and means-tested programs under the Elementary and Secondary Education Act.

What If I Do Not Fulfill My Obligations?

If you do not provide sufficient support to the person who becomes a lawful permanent resident based on a Form I-864 that you signed, that person may sue you for this support.

If a Federal, state, local, or private agency provided any covered means-tested public benefit to the person who becomes a lawful permanent resident based on a Form I-864 that you signed, the agency may ask you to reimburse them for the amount of the benefits they provided. If you do not make the reimbursement, the agency may sue you for the amount that the agency believes you owe.

If you are sued, and the court enters a judgment against you, the person or agency that sued you may use any legally permitted procedures for enforcing or collecting the judgment. You may also be required to pay the costs of collection, including attorney fees.

If you do not file a properly completed Form I-865 within 30 days of any change of address, USCIS may impose a civil fine for your failing to do so.

When Will These Obligations End?

Your obligations under a Form I-864 that you signed will end if the person who becomes a lawful permanent resident based on that affidavit:

A. Becomes a U.S. citizen;

B. Has worked, or can receive credit for, 40 quarters of coverage under the Social Security Act;

C. No longer has lawful permanent resident status and has departed the United States;

D. Is subject to removal, but applies for and obtains, in removal proceedings, a new grant of adjustment of status, based on a new affidavit of support, if one is required; or

E. Dies.

NOTE: Divorce **does not** terminate your obligations under Form I-864.

Your obligations under a Form I-864 that you signed also end if you die. Therefore, if you die, your estate is not required to take responsibility for the person's support after your death. However, your estate may owe any support that you accumulated before you died.

Sponsor's Statement

NOTE: Select the box for either **Item Number 1.a.** or **1.b.** If applicable, select the box for **Item Number 2.**

1.a. [X] I can read and understand English, and have read and understand every question and instruction on this affidavit, as well as my answer to every question.

1.b. [ ] The interpreter named in **Part 9.** has also read to me every question and instruction on this affidavit, as well as my answer to every question, in __________, a language in which I am fluent. I understand every question and instruction on this affidavit as translated to me by my interpreter, and have provided complete, true, and correct responses in the language indicated above.

Part 8. Sponsor's Contract, Statement, Contact Information, Certification, and Signature (continued)

2. [X] I have requested the services of and consented to Brian D Lerner, who [X] is [ ] is not an attorney or accredited representative, preparing this affidavit for me.

Sponsor's Contact Information

3. Sponsor's Daytime Telephone Number

4. Sponsor's Mobile Telephone Number (if any)

5. Sponsor's Email Address (if any)

Sponsor's Certification

Copies of any documents I have submitted are exact photocopies of unaltered, original documents, and I understand that USCIS or the Department of State may require that I submit original documents to USCIS or the Department of State at a later date. Furthermore, I authorize the release of any information from any and all of my records that USCIS or the Department of State may need to determine my eligibility for the benefit that I seek.

I furthermore authorize release of information contained in this affidavit, in supporting documents, and in my USCIS or Department of State records to other entities and persons where necessary for the administration and enforcement of U.S. immigration laws.

I certify, under penalty of perjury, that the information in my affidavit and any document submitted with my affidavit were provided by me and are complete, true, and correct, and:

A. I know the contents of this affidavit of support that I signed;

B. I have read and I understand each of the obligations described in **Part 8.**, and I agree, freely and without any mental reservation or purpose of evasion, to accept each of those obligations in order to make it possible for the immigrants indicated in **Part 3.** to become lawful permanent residents of the United States;

C. I agree to submit to the personal jurisdiction of any Federal or state court that has subject matter jurisdiction of a lawsuit against me to enforce my obligations under this Form I-864;

D. Each of the Federal income tax returns submitted in support of this affidavit are true copies, or are unaltered tax transcripts, of the tax returns I filed with the IRS;

E. I understand that, if I am related to the sponsored immigrant by marriage, the termination of the marriage (by divorce, dissolution, annulment, or other legal process) will not relieve me of my obligations under this Form I-864; and

F. I authorize the Social Security Administration to release information about me in its records to the Department of State and USCIS.

Sponsor's Signature

6.a. Sponsor's Signature

6.b. Date of Signature (mm/dd/yyyy) 10/1/17

NOTE TO ALL SPONSORS: If you do not completely fill out this affidavit or fail to submit required documents listed in the Instructions, USCIS or the Department of State may deny your affidavit.

Part 9. Interpreter's Contact Information, Certification, and Signature

Provide the following information about the interpreter.

Interpreter's Full Name

1.a. Interpreter's Family Name (Last Name)

1.b. Interpreter's Given Name (First Name)

2. Interpreter's Business or Organization Name (if any)

Interpreter's Mailing Address

3.a. Street Number and Name

3.b. ☐ Apt. ☐ Ste. ☐ Flr.

3.c. City or Town

3.d. State **3.e.** ZIP Code

3.f. Province

3.g. Postal Code

3.h. Country

Interpreter's Contact Information

4. Interpreter's Daytime Telephone Number

5. Interpreter's Email Address (if any)

Interpreter's Certification

I certify that:

I am fluent in English and ____________,
which is the same language provided in **Part 8., Item Number 1.b.**;

I have read to this sponsor every question and instruction on this affidavit, as well as the answer to every question, in the language provided in **Part 8., Item Number 1.b.**; and

The sponsor has informed me that he or she understands every instruction and question on the affidavit, as well as the answer to every question, and the sponsor verified the accuracy of every answer.

Interpreter's Signature

6.a. Interpreter's Signature

6.b. Date of Signature (mm/dd/yyyy)

Part 10. Contact Information, Statement, Certification, and Signature of the Person Preparing this Affidavit, If Other Than the Sponsor

Provide the following information about the preparer.

Preparer's Full Name

1.a. Preparer's Family Name (Last Name)

Lerner

1.b. Preparer's Given Name (First Name)

Brian

2. Preparer's Business or Organization Name (if any)

Law Offices of Brian D. Lerner

Part 10. Contact Information, Statement, Certification, and Signature of the Person Preparing this Affidavit, If Other Than the Sponsor (continued)

Preparer's Mailing Address

3.a. Street Number and Name: 3233 E Broadway

3.b. ☐ Apt. ☐ Ste. ☐ Flr.

3.c. City or Town: Long Beach

3.d. State: CA 3.e. ZIP Code: 90803

3.f. Province:

3.g. Postal Code:

3.h. Country: USA

Preparer's Contact Information

4. Preparer's Daytime Telephone Number: 5624950554

5. Preparer's Fax Number: 5626088672

6. Preparer's Email Address (if any): blerner@californiaimmigration.us

Preparer's Statement

7.a. ☐ I am not an attorney or accredited representative but have prepared this affidavit on behalf of the sponsor and with the sponsor's consent.

7.b. ☒ I am an attorney or accredited representative and my representation of the sponsor in this case ☐ extends ☒ does not extend beyond the preparation of this affidavit.

NOTE: If you are an attorney or accredited representative whose representation extends beyond preparation of this affidavit, you must submit a completed Form G-28, Notice of Entry of Appearance as Attorney or Accredited Representative, with this affidavit.

Preparer's Certification

By my signature, I certify, swear, or affirm, under penalty of perjury, that I prepared this affidavit on behalf of, at the request of, and with the express consent of the sponsor. I completed this affidavit based only on responses the sponsor provided to me. After completing the affidavit, I reviewed it and all of the responses with the sponsor, who agreed with every answer on the affidavit. If the sponsor supplied additional information concerning a question on the affidavit, I recorded it on the affidavit.

Preparer's Signature

8.a. Preparer's Signature: [signature]

8.b. Date of Signature (mm/dd/yyyy):

Part 11. Additional Information

If you need extra space to provide any additional information within this affidavit, use the space below. If you need more space than what is provided, you may make copies of this page to complete and file with this affidavit or attach a separate sheet of paper. Include your name and A-Number (if any) at the top of each sheet; indicate the **Page Number; Part Number,** and **Item Number** to which your answer refers; and sign and date each sheet.

Your Full Name

1.a. Family Name (Last Name)

1.b. Given Name (First Name)

1.c. Middle Name

2. A-Number (if any) ▶ A-

3.a. Page Number 3.b. Part Number 3.c. Item Number

3.d.

4.a. Page Number 4.b. Part Number 4.c. Item Number

4.d.

5.a. Page Number 5.b. Part Number 5.c. Item Number

5.d.

EXHIBITS

EXHIBIT '1':
Petitioner's Birth Certificate

CERTIFICATION OF LIVE BIRTH

STATE OF HAWAII
HONOLULU

DEPARTMENT OF HEALTH
HAWAII U.S.A.

CERTIFICATE NO. **151 1976 - 000391**

CHILD'S NAME

DATE OF BIRTH	HOUR OF BIRTH	SEX
January 22, 1976	6:46 AM	FEMALE
CITY, TOWN OR LOCATION OF BIRTH	ISLAND OF BIRTH	COUNTY OF BIRTH
	OAHU	HONOLULU

MOTHER'S MAIDEN NAME

MOTHER'S RACE
JAPANESE, CHINESE

FATHER'S NAME

FATHER'S RACE
JAPANESE

DATE FILED BY REGISTRAR
February 4, 1976

OHSM 1.1 (Rev. 11/01) LASER

This copy serves as prima facie evidence of the fact of birth in any court proceeding. (HRS 338-13(b), 338-19)

ANY ALTERATIONS INVALIDATE THIS CERTIFICATE

EXHIBIT '2':
Petitioner's Passport

We the People
Of the United States,
PASSPORT
PASSEPORT
PASAPORTE
UNITED STATES OF AMERICA
P
USA
425426137
RIOS
UNITED STATES OF AMERICA
22 Jan 1976
HAWAII, U.S.A.
F
03 Oct 2007
United States
02 Oct 2017
Department of State
SEE PAGE 27
USA

EXHIBIT '3':
Applicant's Birth Certificate with English Translation

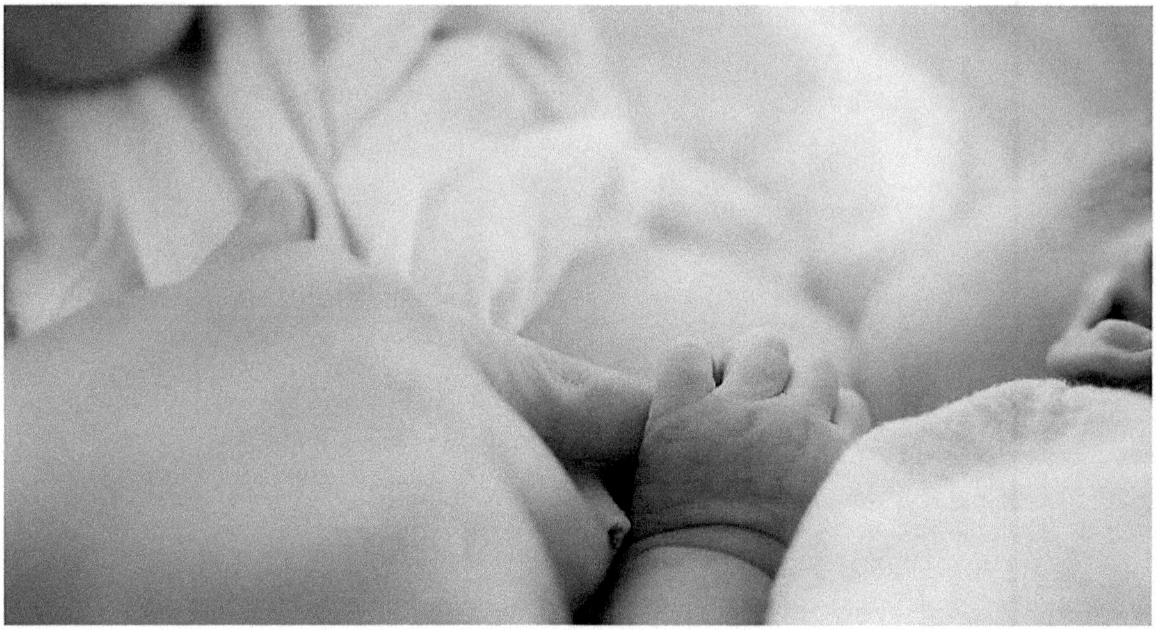

*** English Extract of Spanish Birth Certificate***
Civil Registration

Name of Registered Child:	
Sex:	Male
Date of Birth:	02/24/1980
Place of Birth:	Tepepa, Acaxochitlan, Hidalgo, Mexico
Father of Child:	Martinez,
Nationality of Father:	Mexican
Mother of Child:	
Nationality of Mother:	Mexican

Certificate Information

Issue Date:	06/16/1980
Place of Issue:	Acaxochitlan, Hidalgo, Mexico
Magistrate:	Lechuga Sosa, Erik Antonio
Record Location:	Acaxochitlan, Hidalgo, Mexico
Certificate No.:	No. 00579
Folio:	No. 1651449
Book No.:	02

Translator's Certificate of Competence

I, Elena Valenzuela, certify that the above is an accurate translation of the original Birth Certificate in Spanish and that I am competent in both English and Spanish to render such translation.

Elena Valenzuela　　　　　　　　Date

Law Offices of Brian D. Lerner
3233 East Broadway
Long Beach, CA 90803
Tel: (562) 495-0554

ESTADOS UNIDOS MEXICANOS

EN NOMBRE DEL ESTADO LIBRE Y SOBERANO DE HIDALGO Y COMO OFICIAL DEL REGISTRO DEL ESTADO FAMILIAR, HAGO SABER A LOS QUE LA PRESENTE VEREN, Y CERTIFICO QUE EN EL LIBRO NUMERO 02 DEL REGISTRO QUE ES A MI CARGO A LA FOJA 579 SE ENCUENTRAN ASENTADOS LOS DATOS SIGUIENTES:

ACTA DE NACIMIENTO

CRP:
CURP.

OFICIALIA	LIBRO No	ACTA No.	LOCALIDAD	FECHA DE REGISTRO
01	02	00579	ACAXOCHITLAN	DIA MES AÑO 10/JUNIO/1980

MUNICIPIO O DELEGACION	ENTIDAD FEDERATIVA
ACAXOCHITLAN	HIDALGO

DATOS DEL REGISTRADO

NOMBRE(S) — PRIMER APELLIDO — SEGUNDO APELLIDO

MEXICANA — MASCULINO

NACIONALIDAD — SEXO

LUGAR Y FECHA DE NACIMIENTO

LOCALIDAD	MUNICIPIO	ENTIDAD	PAIS	FECHA
TEPEPA	ACAXOCHITLAN	HIDALGO	MEXICO	24/FEBRERO/1980

COMPARECIO: EL PADRE

DATOS DE LOS PADRES

MARTINEZ

NOMBRE(S) — PRIMER APELLIDO — SEGUNDO APELLIDO

MEXICANA

NACIONALIDAD

LIBORIA — HERNANDEZ

NOMBRE(S) — PRIMER APELLIDO — SEGUNDO APELLIDO

MEXICANA

NACIONALIDAD

DATOS DE LOS ABUELOS

ABUELO PATERNO: (FINADO) NACIONALIDAD: MEXICANA

ABUELA PATERNA: (FINADA) NACIONALIDAD: MEXICANA

ABUELO MATERNO: NACIONALIDAD: MEXICANA

ABUELA MATERNA: NACIONALIDAD: MEXICANA

SE EXTIENDE ESTA CERTIFICACION EN CUMPLIMIENTO DEL ARTICULO 386 DEL CODIGO FAMILIAR VIGENTE EN EL ESTADO, EN ACAXOCHITLAN, HGO. EL SUSCRITO OFICIAL DEL REGISTRO DEL ESTADO FAMILIAR

REGISTRO DEL ESTADO FAMILIAR * ACAXOCHITLAN HGO

2006 - 2009

1651449

LIC. ERIK ANTONIO LECHUGA SOSA
OFICIAL DEL REGISTRO DEL ESTADO FAMILIAR

18/01/2007 10:20:60
FECHA DE EXPEDICION

EXHIBIT '4':
Applicant's Marriage Certificate with English Translation

*** English Extract of Spanish Marriage Certificate***
Civil Registration

Groom's Name:	(Sex: Male)
Birth Date:	02/24/1980
Birth Place:	Tepepa, Acaxochitlan, Hidalgo, Mexico
Nationality:	Mexican
Father's Name:	Martinez,
Nationality:	Mexican
Mother's Name:	Hernandez,
Nationality:	Mexican
Bride's Name:	Ige, (Sex: Famale)
Birth Date:	01/22/1976
Birth Place:	Honolulu, Hawaii
Nationality:	American
Father's Name:	Ige, Stanley Tasuku
Nationality:	American
Mother's Name:	Chung, Carol Yayote
Nationality:	American

Certificate Information

Issue Date:	07/28/2005
Place of Issue:	Tulancingo, Hidalgo, Mexico
Magistrate:	Islas Lopez, Ricardo
Record Location:	Book No. 2 / Certificate No. 371
Certificate No.:	146579

Translator's Certificate of Competence

I, Elena Valenzuela, certify that the above is an accurate translation of the original Marriage Certificate in Spanish and that I am competent in both English and Spanish to render such translation.

Elena Valenzuela   11/12/15
Elena Valenzuela   Date

Law Offices of Brian D. Lerner
3233 E Broadway Avenue Long Beach, CA 90803
Tel: (562) 495-0554

ESTADOS UNIDOS MEXICANOS
ESTADO LIBRE Y SOBERANO DE HIDALGO
REGISTRO DEL ESTADO FAMILIAR

146579

EL	CRIP:
	CURP:
ELLA	CRIP:
	CURP:

PODER EJECUTIVO — ACTA DE MATRIMONIO

OFICIALIA	LIBRO No.	ACTA No.	FOJA No.	LOCALIDAD	FECHA DE REGISTRO DIA MES AÑO
1	2	171	171	TULANCINGO	20/07/2005

MUNICIPIO: TULANCINGO
ENTIDAD FEDERATIVA: HIDALGO

DATOS DE LOS CONTRAYENTES

NOMBRE DEL CONTRAYENTE: [redacted] (NOMBRE(S)) ROLDAN (PRIMER APELLIDO) [redacted] (SEGUNDO APELLIDO)
LUGAR DE NACIMIENTO: TEPEPA (LOCALIDAD) ACAXOCHITLAN (MUNICIPIO) HIDALGO (ENTIDAD FEDERATIVA) MEXICO (PAIS)
EDAD: 26 AÑOS FECHA DE NACIMIENTO: 24/02/1980 NACIONALIDAD: MEXICANA
DOMICILIO HABITUAL: LOC. TEPEPA S/N BARRIO HUITZILINGO ACAXOCHITLAN, HIDALGO
OCUPACION: EMPLEADO

NOMBRE DE LA CONTRAYENTE: [redacted] (NOMBRE(S)) IGE (PRIMER APELLIDO) (SEGUNDO APELLIDO)
LUGAR DE NACIMIENTO: (LOCALIDAD) HONOLULU (MUNICIPIO) HAWAII (ENTIDAD FEDERATIVA) U.S.A. (PAIS)
EDAD: 29 AÑOS FECHA DE NACIMIENTO: 22/01/1976 NACIONALIDAD: AMERICANA
DOMICILIO HABITUAL: 1008 MANA'IKI PLACE HONOLULU HAWAII, U.S.A.
OCUPACION: GERENTE

PADRES DEL CONTRAYENTE

NOMBRE DEL PADRE: [redacted] ROLDAN RIOS FINADO NACIONALIDAD: MEXICANA
DOMICILIO:
NOMBRE DE LA MADRE: LIBORIA RIOS HERNANDEZ NACIONALIDAD: MEXICANA
DOMICILIO: TULANCINGO, HIDALGO

PADRES DE LA CONTRAYENTE

NOMBRE DEL PADRE: STANLEY TASUKU IGE NACIONALIDAD: AMERICANA
DOMICILIO: HAWAII, U.S.A.
NOMBRE DE LA MADRE: CAROL YAYOI K CHUNG NACIONALIDAD: AMERICANA
DOMICILIO: HAWAII U.S.A.

TESTIGOS DE LOS CONTRAYENTES

NOMBRE: [redacted] NACIONALIDAD: MEXICANA EDAD: 11 AÑOS
DOMICILIO: TULANCINGO, HIDALGO
PARENTESCO: HERMANO
NOMBRE: [redacted] NACIONALIDAD: MEXICANA EDAD: 63 AÑOS
DOMICILIO: ACAXOCHITLAN, HIDALGO
PARENTESCO: NINGUNO
NOMBRE: JOVITA [redacted] NACIONALIDAD: MEXICANA EDAD: 22 AÑOS
DOMICILIO: TULANCINGO, HIDALGO
PARENTESCO: NINGUNO
NOMBRE: [redacted] NACIONALIDAD: MEXICANA EDAD: 31 AÑOS
DOMICILIO:
PARENTESCO: NINGUNO

NOMBRE(S) DE LA(S) PERSONA(S) QUE DA(N) SU CONSENTIMIENTO POR MINORIA DE EDAD DEL(OS) CONTRAYENTE(S)

AUTORIZACION DE LA SECRETARIA DE GOBERNACION EN CASO DE CONTRAYENTE(S) EXTRANJERO(S)

ESTE MATRIMONIO QUEDA SUJETO AL REGIMEN DE: SOCIEDAD CONYUGAL

HUELLA DIGITAL DEL CONTRAYENTE — CONTRAYENTES — HUELLA DIGITAL DE LA CONTRAYENTE

PADRES

TESTIGOS

SELLO

EL C. Oficial No. 01 del Registro del Estado Familiar

LIC. RICARDO ISLAS LOPEZ
nombre — firma

INTERESADO

EXHIBIT '5':
Applicant's Passport

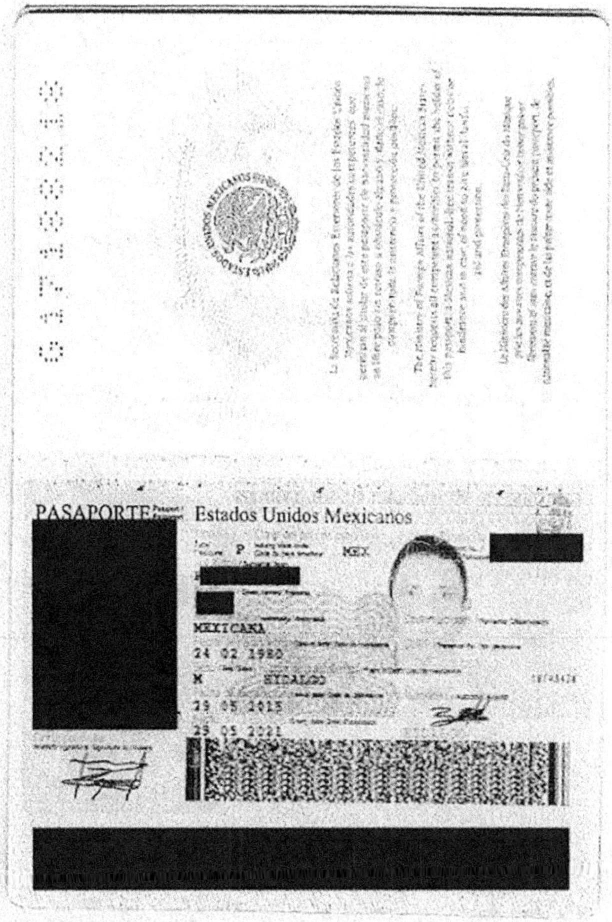
PASAPORTE
Estados Unidos Mexicanos
MEX
MEXICANA
24 02 1980
29 05 2015
29 05 2021

EXHIBIT '6':
Proof of Relationship between Petitioner and Applicant

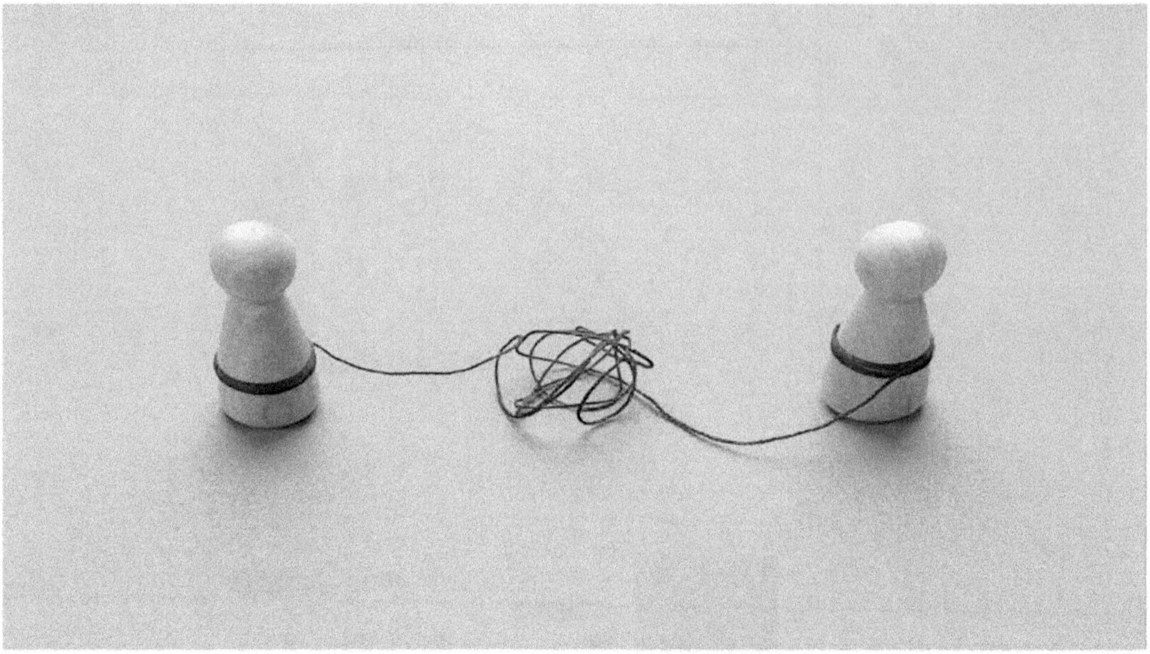

12/19/2010

12/18/2011

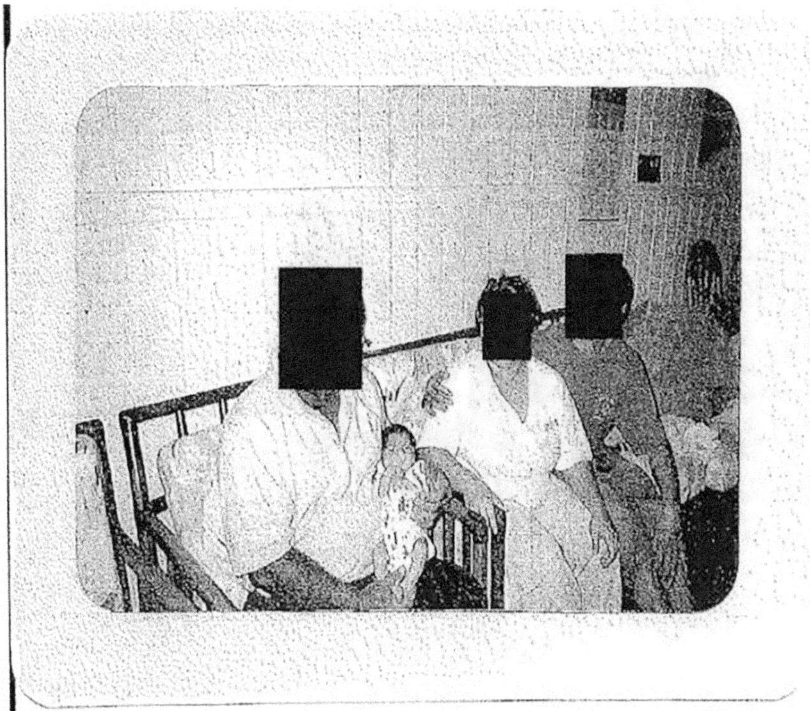

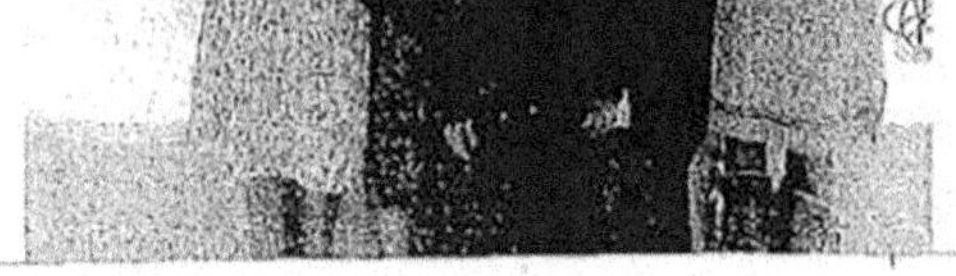

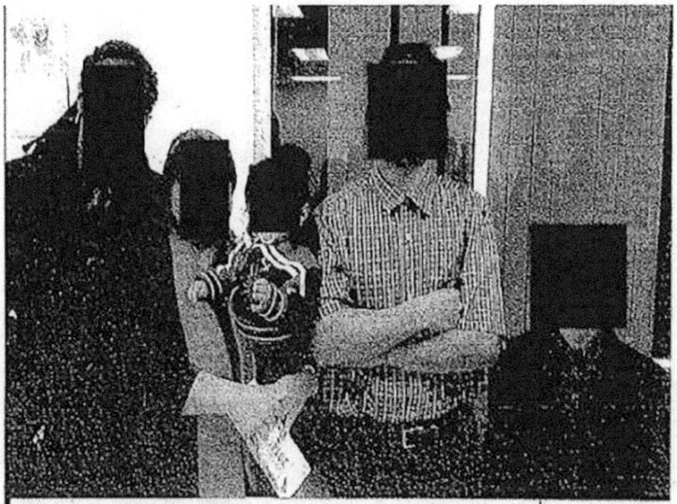

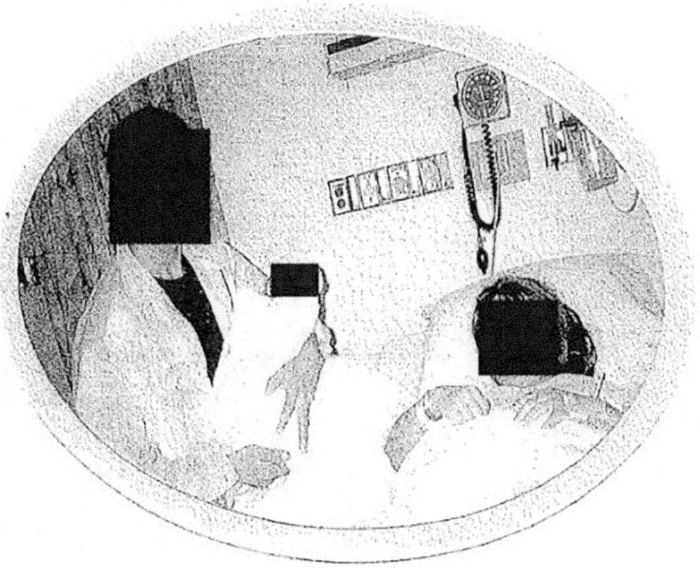

CERTIFICATE OF LIVE BIRTH

STATE OF HAWAII
DEPARTMENT OF HEALTH

CERTIFICATE NO. **151 2012 - 014913**

DATE OF BIRTH October 9, 2012	HOUR OF BIRTH 8:24AM	SEX MALE
CITY, TOWN OR LOCATION OF BIRTH HONOLULU	ISLAND OF BIRTH OAHU	COUNTY OF BIRTH HONOLULU
M... MAID... IGE		
MOTHER'S RACE JAPANESE		MOTHER'S STATE/COUNTRY OF BIRTH HAWAII
FATHER'S NAME		
FATHER'S RACE MEXICAN		FATHER'S STATE/COUNTRY OF BIRTH MEXICO
DATE FILED BY REGISTRAR October 15, 2012		

OHSM 1.1 (Rev 10/08) LASER This copy serves as prima facie evidence of the fact of birth in any court proceeding. [HRS 338-13(b), 338-19] 2428450

ANY ALTERATIONS INVALIDATE THIS CERTIFICATE

8/25/2017

CERTIFICATION OF LIVE BIRTH

STATE OF HAWAII
HONOLULU

DEPARTMENT OF HEALTH
HAWAII U.S.A.

CERTIFICATE NO. **151 2005 - 002695**

CHILD'S NAME

DATE OF BIRTH	HOUR OF BIRTH	SEX
March 1, 2005	2:05 PM	MALE

CITY, TOWN OR LOCATION OF BIRTH	ISLAND OF BIRTH	COUNTY OF BIRTH
HILO	HAWAII	HAWAII

MOTHER'S MAIDEN NAME

MOTHER'S RACE
JAPANESE

FATHER'S NAME

FATHER'S RACE
MEXICAN

DATE FILED BY REGISTRAR
March 4,2005

OHSM 1.1 (Rev 11/01) LASER

This copy serves as prima facie evidence of the fact of birth in any court proceeding. [HRS 338-13(b), 338-19]

ANY ALTERATIONS INVALIDATE THIS CERTIFICATE

EXHIBIT '7':

Proof of Payment of Immigrant Visa Fee

U.S. DEPARTMENT of STATE
CONSULAR ELECTRONIC APPLICATION CENTER

Payment Receipts for IV Case CDJ2016801007
IV Fee Payment Receipt Details

Principal Applicant
Payment of Services Initiated 23-JAN-2017 20:30:57
Payment Processed Date 24-JAN-2017
Payment Amount $325.00
Payer K
Payer Email yahoo.com
Transaction ID 2608HLJG

Applicant	IV Fee Payment Status	Fee Amount
	PAID	$325.00

Next Steps

If your payment status shows that it is IN PROCESS, wait two to three business days for the payment to clear. Then sign into the system again to check for a status update.

If your payment status shows a status other than IN PROCESS or PAID, sign in to the Immigrant Visa Invoice Payment Center page https://ceac.state.gov/CTRAC/Invoice/Signon.aspx and click on Get Help.

If you receive a notice that your case has entered termination, do not attempt to pay any fees. You must contact the National Visa Center (NVC) immediately to resume processing of your petition. You can find NVC contact information at nvc.state.gov/ask

When the IV fee payment status is PAID:

1. Each applicant must complete and submit an Online Immigrant Visa and Alien Registration Application (DS-260). To submit your application, go to http://ceac.state.gov/iv, and sign in. Read the Summary Information. Click on the IV APPLICATION tab and follow the application instructions.
2. To review specific U.S. Embassy or Consulate instructions and options that may apply to your case, go to nvc.state.gov/document. You will find the information in a downloadable PDF format at the bottom of the page.
3. To complete your Immigrant Visa Application, you must submit copies of all supporting documents. Go to nvc.state.gov/submit. You will find instructions if you are required to email your documents, as well as the processing and mailing information.
4. If you are required to submit physical copies of your documents, you must include a barcoded cover sheet to identify your documents.

- If you received an Instruction Packet from the NVC, it contains a cover sheet. You can send that cover sheet or a copy of the cover sheet.
- If you need a new cover sheet, print one by clicking the Print Document Cover Sheet button on the Receipt page.
- If you cannot print a cover sheet, click the Email Document Cover Sheet button.

Then send an electronic copy to an email address where you can print it.

IMPORTANT NOTES:

- If you decide to file Form I-601A, Application for Provisional Unlawful Presence Waiver with USCIS, you must include a copy of this fee payment receipt or USCIS will reject your Form I-601A.
- Please keep this receipt for your records. If you can't print the receipt now, return to the Receipt Screen and email a copy to an address where you can print it later.
- Do not let more than one-year pass without contacting the NVC about your immigrant visa petition. If a period of one-year passes from the last date of contact, all submitted forms and fees will expire and you must resubmit them to resume processing.
- You will find the next steps about AOS fee payments on the AOS fee payment receipt.

U.S. DEPARTMENT of STATE
CONSULAR ELECTRONIC APPLICATION CENTER

Payment Receipts for IV Case CDJ2016801007
AOS Fee Payment Receipt Details

Payment Status PAID
Principal Applicant [redacted]
Petitioner [redacted]
Payment Amount $120.00
Payment of Services Initiated 23-JAN-2017 20:28:30
Payment Processed Date 24-JAN-2017
Payer [redacted] K
Payer Email [redacted]
Transaction ID 2608HKI2

Next Steps

If your payment status shows that it is IN PROCESS, wait two to three business days for the payment to clear. Then sign into the system again to check for a status update.

If your payment status shows a status other than IN PROCESS or PAID, sign in to the Immigrant Visa Invoice Payment Center page https://ceac.state.gov/CTRAC/Invoice/Signon.aspx and click on Get Help.

If you receive a notice that your case has entered termination, do not attempt to pay any fees. You must contact the National Visa Center (NVC) immediately to resume processing of your petition. You can find NVC contact information at nvc.state.gov/ask.

To review specific U.S. Embassy or Consulate instructions and options that may apply to your case, go to nvc.state.gov/document. You will find the information in a downloadable PDF format at the bottom of the page.

When the AOS fee payment status is PAID:

1. The petitioner must complete and submit an Affidavit of Support (Form I-864). To submit your application, go to nvc.state.gov/aos.
2. Read the introductory paragraph. Then click on > Complete an Affidavit of Support form. From the chart, select the form that fits your situation. You will need to click the GO button to access the form and instructions.
3. To complete your Immigrant Visa Application, you must submit copies of all supporting documents. Go to nvc.state.gov/submit. You will find instructions if you are required to email your documents, as well as the processing and mailing information.
4. If you are required to submit physical copies of your documents, you must include a barcoded cover sheet to identify your documents.

- If you received an Instruction Packet from the NVC, it contains a cover sheet. You can send that cover sheet or a copy of the cover sheet.
- If you need a new cover sheet, print one by clicking the Print Document Cover Sheet button on the Receipt page.
- If you cannot print a cover sheet, click the Email Document Cover Sheet button.

Then send an electronic copy to an email address where you can print it.

You will find steps concerning IV fee payments on the IV fee payment receipt.

EXHIBIT '8':
Confirmation of DS-260 Immigrant Visa Electronic Application

U.S. DEPARTMENT of STATE
CONSULAR ELECTRONIC APPLICATION CENTER

Online Immigrant Visa and Alien Registration Application (DS-260)

Immigrant Visa and Alien Registration Application Confirmation

Thank You

You have successfully submitted an Immigrant Visa and Alien Registration Application (Form DS-260). You must bring to your visa interview proof that you submitted this form by printing a confirmation page using the below button. Do not print a copy of this screen; use the below PRINT CONFIRMATION button to print a page with a unique barcode related to your visa application. You can print a confirmation from this website at any time.

Next Step

Your Immigrant Visa and Alien Registration Application (Form DS-260) was sent to the National Visa Center (NVC) for review. **However, NVC will not review your Form DS-260 until they have received the required financial and civil documents that you must also submit.** If you have not sent NVC those items, please do so now. Visit http://nvc.state.gov (English) or http://nvc.state.gov/espanol (Spanish) and review Steps 4-6 for instructions.

When NVC has your DS-260, financial documents, **and** civil documents, they will review these items. Please allow 30 days for NVC to complete their review. If the documents you submit are insufficient or incomplete, NVC will send instructions on how to correct your submission. **NVC cannot schedule your visa interview until your supporting documentation is complete.**

Your Visa Interview

Once you have a visa interview appointment, you need to:

1. Obtain and submit photographs that meet the Department of State's visa requirements.
2. Review the information for the U.S. Embassy where your visa interview will occur.

Please use the buttons below for information on these items as well as instructions for submitting documents to NVC.

During the interview with a consular officer, you will be required to sign your application by providing a "biometric signature" -- in other words, your fingerprints. By providing this biometric signature, you are certifying under penalty of perjury that you have read and understood the questions in your immigrant visa application. You are also certifying that all statements that appear in your immigrant visa application have been made by you and are true and complete to the best of your knowledge and belief. At the time of your interview, you will also be required to certify under penalty of perjury that all statements in your application and those made during your interview are true and complete to the best of your knowledge and belief.

This confirms the submission of the Immigrant Visa and Alien Registration application for:

Name Provided:	
Country/Region of Origin (Nationality):	
Completed On:	14 AUG 2017
Case No:	CDJ2016801007
Confirmation No:	AA006ZINV8

C D J 2 0 1 6 8 0 1 0 0 7

A A 0 0 6 Z I N V 8

THIS IS NOT A VISA

Version 01.01.00

EXHIBIT '9':

Correction Sheet of DS-260 Immigrant Visa Electronic Application

Department of Homeland Security
U.S. Citizenship and Immigration Services

I-797, Notice of Action

THE UNITED STATES OF AMERICA

RECEIPT NUMBER LIN-16-906-04959		CASE TYPE I130 PETITION FOR ALIEN RELATIVE
RECEIPT DATE April 22, 2016	PRIORITY DATE April 18, 2016	PETITIONER
NOTICE DATE September 20, 2016	PAGE 1 of 1	BENEFICIARY A096 214 149

BRIAN D LERNER
LAW OFFICES OF BRIAN D LERNER
3233 E BROADWAY
LONG BEACH CA 90803

Notice Type: Approval Notice
Section: Husband or wife of U.S. Citizen, 201(b) INA

The above petition has been approved. We have sent the original visa petition to the Department of State National Visa Center (NVC), 32 Rochester Avenue, Portsmouth, NH 03801-2909. NVC processes all approved immigrant visa petitions that need consular action. It also determines which consular post is the appropriate consulate to complete visa processing. NVC will then forward the approved petition to that consulate.

The NVC will contact the person for whom you are petitioning(beneficiary) concerning further immigrant visa processing steps.

You should allow a minimum of 30 days for Department of State processing before contacting the NVC. If you have not received any correspondence from the NVC within 30 days, you may contact the NVC by e-mail at NVCINQUIRY@state.gov. You will need to enter the USCIS receipt number from this approval notice in the subject line. In order to receive information about your petition, you will need to include the Petitioner's name and date of birth, and the Applicant's name and date of birth, in the body of the e-mail.

The approval of this visa petition does not in itself grant any immigration status and does not guarantee that the alien beneficiary will subsequently be found to be eligible for a visa, for admission to the United States, or for an extension, change, or adjustment of status.

THIS FORM IS NOT A VISA AND MAY NOT BE USED IN PLACE OF A VISA.

NOTICE: Although this application/petition has been approved, USCIS and the U.S. Department of Homeland Security reserve the right to verify the information submitted in this application, petition and/or supporting documentation to ensure conformity with applicable laws, rules, regulations, and other authorities. Methods used for verifying information may include, but are not limited to, the review of public information and records, contact by correspondence, the internet, or telephone, and site inspections of businesses and residences. Information obtained during the course of verification will be used to determine whether revocation, rescission, and/or removal proceedings are appropriate. Applicants, petitioners, and representatives of record will be provided an opportunity to address derogatory information before any formal proceeding is initiated.

Please see the additional information on the back. You will be notified separately about any other cases you filed.

USCIS
TEXAS SERVICE CENTER
P O BOX 851488 - DEPT A
MESQUITE TX 75185-1488
Customer Service Telephone: (800) 375-5283

EXHIBIT '10':

I-130 Approval Notice of Applicant and Petitioner

FORM **W-2 Wage and Tax Statement**

Copy C For EMPLOYEE'S RECORDS (See notice on back of Copy 2)

Dept. of the Treasury • Internal Revenue Service

This information is being furnished to the Internal Revenue Service. If you are required to file a tax return, a negligence penalty or other sanction may be imposed on you if this income is taxable and you fail to report it.

These substitute W-2 Wage and Tax Statements are acceptable for filing with your Federal, State and Local Income Tax Returns.
If you worked in multiple locations, or had several forms of special compensation, you may receive more than one of these documents.

The white copies of the W-2 forms are for your tax returns; the blue copy is for your records. General instructions, including an explanation of the letter codes in box 12, are on the other side of the page.

To the right is an explanation of your W-2 wages. Please note that the Gross amount may include adjustments.

	Federal Box 1	Social Security Box 3 & 7	Medicare Box 5	State Box 16	Local Box 18
Gross	38644.61	38644.61	38644.61	38644.61	
Deferred Comp.	2181.32-			2181.32-	
Sect. 125 Plan	1192.79-	1192.79-	1192.79-	1192.79-	
W-2 Wages	35270.50	37451.82	37451.82	35270.50	

Control number	01HN021278
	2016
OMB NO.	1545-0008
Employer identification number	99-0073436
Employer's name, address, and ZIP code	HAWAIIUSA FEDERAL CREDIT UNION 1226 COLLEGE WALK HONOLULU HI 96817
Employee's first name and initial / Last name	CHELSIE K RIOS
Employee's address	1808 MANAIKI PL HONOLULU, HI 96819
1 Wages, tips, other compensation	35270.50
2 Federal income tax withheld	1830.35
3 Social security wages	37451.82
4 Social security tax withheld	2322.01
5 Medicare wages and tips	37451.82
6 Medicare tax withheld	543.05
13 Retirement plan	X
12	D 2181.32 DD 15216.78
15 State	HI
16 State wages, tips, etc.	35270.50
17 State income tax	1620.38

FOLD AND TEAR ALONG PERFORATION

Control number	01HN021278
OMB NO.	1545-0008
Employer's name, address, and ZIP code	HAWAIIUSA FEDERAL CREDIT UNION 1226 COLLEGE WALK HONOLULU HI 96817
Employee's first name and initial / Last name	CHELSIE K RIOS
1 Wages, tips, other compensation	35270.50
2 Federal income tax withheld	1830.35
3 Social security wages	37451.82
4 Social security tax withheld	2322.01
5 Medicare wages and tips	37451.82
6 Medicare tax withheld	543.05
12	D 2181.32 DD 15216.78
13 Retirement plan	X
15 State	HI
16 State wages, tips, etc.	35270.50
17 State income tax	1620.38

Copy 2 To be filed with Employee's STATE, CITY or LOCAL tax return

Form **W-2 Wage and Tax Statement** 2016

Dept. of the Treasury - Internal Revenue Service

Form **1040A** Department of the Treasury—Internal Revenue Service **U.S. Individual Income Tax Return** (99) **2016** IRS Use Only—Do not write or staple in this space.

Your first name and initial	Last name	OMB No. 1545-0074
K.		Your social security number
If a joint return, spouse's first name and initial	Last name	Spouse's social security number
Home address (number and street). If you have a P.O. box, see instructions.	Apt. no.	▲ Make sure the SSN(s) above
City, town or post office, state, and ZIP code. If you have a foreign address, also complete spaces below (see instructions). Honolulu, HI 96819		Presidential Election Campaign Check here if you, or your spouse if filing jointly, want $3 to go to this fund. Checking a box below will not change your tax or refund. ☐ You ☐ Spouse
Foreign country name	Foreign province/state/county	Foreign postal code

Filing status Check only one box.

1 ☐ Single
2 ☐ Married filing jointly (even if only one had income)
3 ☐ Married filing separately. Enter spouse's SSN above and full name here. ▶
4 ☑ Head of household (with qualifying person). (See instructions.) If the qualifying person is a child but not your dependent, enter this child's name here. ▶
5 ☐ Qualifying widow(er) with dependent child (see instructions)

Exemptions

6a ☐ **Yourself.** If someone can claim you as a dependent, **do not** check box 6a.
b ☐ **Spouse**

Boxes checked on 6a and 6b: 1

c **Dependents:** (If more than six dependents, see instructions.)

(1) First name / Last name	(2) Dependent's social security number	(3) Dependent's relationship to you	(4) ✓ if child under age 17 qualifying for child tax credit (see instructions)
		Son	☑
		Son	☑
			☐
			☐
			☐
			☐

No. of children on 6c who:
• lived with you: 2
• did not live with you due to divorce or separation (see instructions):
Dependents on 6c not entered above:

d Total number of exemptions claimed. Add numbers on lines above ▶ 3

Income

Attach Form(s) W-2 here. Also attach Form(s) 1099-R if tax was withheld. If you did not get a W-2, see instructions.

7	Wages, salaries, tips, etc. Attach Form(s) W-2.		7	35721	00
8a	Taxable interest. Attach Schedule B if required.		8a	0	
b	**Tax-exempt** interest. **Do not** include on line 8a.	8b			
9a	Ordinary dividends. Attach Schedule B if required.		9a	0	
b	Qualified dividends (see instructions).	9b			
10	Capital gain distributions (see instructions).		10	0	
11a	IRA distributions. 11a	11b Taxable amount (see instructions).	11b	0	
12a	Pensions and annuities. 12a	12b Taxable amount (see instructions).	12b	0	
13	Unemployment compensation and Alaska Permanent Fund dividends.		13	0	
14a	Social security benefits. 14a	14b Taxable amount (see instructions).	14b	0	
15	Add lines 7 through 14b (far right column). This is your **total income.** ▶		15	35271	00

Adjusted gross income

16	Educator expenses (see instructions).	16	0			
17	IRA deduction (see instructions).	17	0			
18	Student loan interest deduction (see instructions).	18	0			
19	Tuition and fees. Attach Form 8917.	19	0			
20	Add lines 16 through 19. These are your **total adjustments.**			20	35271	00
21	Subtract line 20 from line 15. This is your **adjusted gross income.** ▶			21	35271	00

For Disclosure, Privacy Act, and Paperwork Reduction Act Notice, see separate instructions. Cat. No. 11327A Form **1040A** (2016)

Form 1040A (2016) Page 2

Tax, credits, and payments

22	Enter the amount from line 21 (adjusted gross income).			22	35271 00
23a	Check if: ☐ You were born before January 2, 1952, ☐ Blind; ☐ Spouse was born before January 2, 1952, ☐ Blind. Total boxes checked ▶ 23a	0			
b	If you are married filing separately and your spouse itemizes deductions, check here ▶ 23b ☐				
24	Enter your **standard deduction**.			24	9300 00
25	Subtract line 24 from line 22. If line 24 is more than line 22, enter -0-.			25	25971 00
26	**Exemptions.** Multiply $4,050 by the number on line 6d.			26	12150 00
27	Subtract line 26 from line 25. If line 26 is more than line 25, enter -0-. This is your **taxable income**.			▶ 27	13821 00
28	Tax, including any alternative minimum tax (see instructions).	28	1411 00		
29	Excess advance premium tax credit repayment. Attach Form 8962.	29	0		
30	Add lines 28 and 29.			30	1411 00
31	Credit for child and dependent care expenses. Attach Form 2441.	31	720 00		
32	Credit for the elderly or the disabled. Attach Schedule R.	32	0		
33	Education credits from Form 8863, line 19.	33	0		
34	Retirement savings contributions credit. Attach Form 8880.	34	0		
35	Child tax credit. Attach Schedule 8812, if required.	35	581 00		
36	Add lines 31 through 35. These are your **total credits**.			36	1301 00
37	Subtract line 36 from line 30. If line 36 is more than line 30, enter -0-.			37	110 00
38	Health care: individual responsibility (see instructions). Full-year coverage ☑			38	
39	Add line 37 and line 38. This is your **total tax**.			39	110 00
40	Federal income tax withheld from Forms W-2 and 1099.	40	1830 00		
41	2016 estimated tax payments and amount applied from 2015 return.	41	0		
42a	**Earned income credit (EIC).**	42a	1974 00		
b	Nontaxable combat pay election. 42b				
43	Additional child tax credit. Attach Schedule 8812.	43	1419 00		
44	American opportunity credit from Form 8863, line 8.	44	0		
45	Net premium tax credit. Attach Form 8962.	45	0		
46	Add lines 40, 41, 42a, 43, 44, and 45. These are your **total payments**.			▶ 46	5223 00

Standard Deduction for—
- People who check any box on line 23a or 23b or who can be claimed as a dependent, see instructions.
- All others: Single or Married filing separately, $6,300; Married filing jointly or Qualifying widow(er), $12,600; Head of household, $9,300

If you have a qualifying child, attach Schedule EIC.

Refund

47	If line 46 is more than line 39, subtract line 39 from line 46. This is the amount you overpaid.	47	5113 00
48a	**Amount of line 47 you want refunded to you.** If Form 8888 is attached, check here ▶ ☐	48a	5113 00
▶ b	Routing number: 3 2 1 3 7 9 4 1 0 ▶ c Type: ☑ Checking ☐ Savings		
▶ d	Account number: 1 1 1 0 1 0 4 5 6 8 0		
49	Amount of line 47 you want applied to your 2017 estimated tax.	49	

Direct deposit? See instructions and fill in 48b, 48c, and 48d or Form 8888.

Amount you owe

50	**Amount you owe.** Subtract line 46 from line 39. For details on how to pay, see instructions.	▶ 50	
51	Estimated tax penalty (see instructions).	51	

Third party designee

Do you want to allow another person to discuss this return with the IRS (see instructions)? ☐ Yes. Complete the following. ☐ No

Designee's name ▶ Phone no. ▶ Personal identification number (PIN) ▶

Sign here

Under penalties of perjury, I declare that I have examined this return and accompanying schedules and statements, and to the best of my knowledge and belief, they are true, correct, and accurately list all amounts and sources of income I received during the tax year. Declaration of preparer (other than the taxpayer) is based on all information of which the preparer has any knowledge.

Joint return? See instructions. Keep a copy for your records.

Your signature	Date	Your occupation	Daytime phone number
	2/26/17	Bank Clerk	808 845 1049
Spouse's signature. If a joint return, both must sign.	Date	Spouse's occupation	If the IRS sent you an Identity Protection PIN, enter it here (see inst.)

Paid preparer use only

Print/type preparer's name	Preparer's signature	Date	Check ▶ ☐ if self-employed	PTIN
Firm's name ▶			Firm's EIN ▶	
Firm's address ▶			Phone no.	

Form **1040A** (2016)

SCHEDULE EIC
(Form 1040A or 1040)

Department of the Treasury
Internal Revenue Service (99)

Earned Income Credit

Qualifying Child Information

1040A
1040

▶ Complete and attach to Form 1040A or 1040 only if you have a qualifying child.

▶ Information about Schedule EIC (Form 1040A or 1040) and its instructions is at www.irs.gov/scheduleeic.

OMB No. 1545-0074

2016

Attachment Sequence No. 43

Name(s) shown on return: [redacted] K. [redacted]

Your social security number: [redacted]

Before you begin:

- See the instructions for Form 1040A, lines 42a and 42b, or Form 1040, lines 66a and 66b, to make sure that (a) you can take the EIC, and (b) you have a qualifying child.
- Be sure the child's name on line 1 and social security number (SSN) on line 2 agree with the child's social security card. Otherwise, at the time we process your return, we may reduce or disallow your EIC. If the name or SSN on the child's social security card is not correct, call the Social Security Administration at 1-800-772-1213.

- *You can't claim the EIC for a child who didn't live with you for more than half of the year.*
- *If you take the EIC even though you are not eligible, you may not be allowed to take the credit for up to 10 years. See the instructions for details.*
- *It will take us longer to process your return and issue your refund if you do not fill in all lines that apply for each qualifying child.*

Qualifying Child Information	Child 1	Child 2	Child 3
1 Child's name If you have more than three qualifying children, you have to list only three to get the maximum credit.	First name / Last name [redacted]	First name / Last name [redacted]	First name / Last name
2 Child's SSN The child must have an SSN as defined in the instructions for Form 1040A, lines 42a and 42b, or Form 1040, lines 66a and 66b, unless the child was born and died in 2016. If your child was born and died in 2016 and did not have an SSN, enter "Died" on this line and attach a copy of the child's birth certificate, death certificate, or hospital medical records.	[redacted]	[redacted]	
3 Child's year of birth	Year 2 0 0 5 *If born after 1997 and the child is younger than you (or your spouse, if filing jointly), skip lines 4a and 4b; go to line 5.*	Year 2 0 1 2 *If born after 1997 and the child is younger than you (or your spouse, if filing jointly), skip lines 4a and 4b; go to line 5.*	Year ____ *If born after 1997 and the child is younger than you (or your spouse, if filing jointly), skip lines 4a and 4b; go to line 5.*
4 a Was the child under age 24 at the end of 2016, a student, and younger than you (or your spouse, if filing jointly)?	☐ Yes. *Go to line 5.* ☐ No. *Go to line 4b.*	☐ Yes. *Go to line 5.* ☐ No. *Go to line 4b.*	☐ Yes. *Go to line 5.* ☐ No. *Go to line 4b.*
b Was the child permanently and totally disabled during any part of 2016?	☐ Yes. *Go to line 5.* ☐ No. The child is not a qualifying child.	☐ Yes. *Go to line 5.* ☐ No. The child is not a qualifying child.	☐ Yes. *Go to line 5.* ☐ No. The child is not a qualifying child.
5 Child's relationship to you (for example, son, daughter, grandchild, niece, nephew, foster child, etc.)	Son	Son	
6 Number of months child lived with you in the United States during 2016 • If the child lived with you for more than half of 2016 but less than 7 months, enter "7." • If the child was born or died in 2016 and your home was the child's home for more than half the time he or she was alive during 2016, enter "12."	12 months *Do not enter more than 12 months.*	12 months *Do not enter more than 12 months.*	____ months *Do not enter more than 12 months.*

For Paperwork Reduction Act Notice, see your tax return instructions. Cat. No. 13339M Schedule EIC (Form 1040A or 1040) 2016

SCHEDULE 8812
(Form 1040A or 1040)

Department of the Treasury
Internal Revenue Service (99)

Child Tax Credit

▶ Attach to Form 1040, Form 1040A, or Form 1040NR.
▶ Information about Schedule 8812 and its separate instructions is at www.irs.gov/schedule8812.

1040 / 1040A / 1040NR / 8812

OMB No. 1545-0074
2016
Attachment Sequence No. 47

Name(s) shown on return: [redacted] K [redacted] | Your social security number: [redacted]

Part I — Filers Who Have Certain Child Dependent(s) with an ITIN (Individual Taxpayer Identification Number)

CAUTION: *Complete this part only for each dependent who has an ITIN and for whom you are claiming the child tax credit. If your dependent is not a qualifying child for the credit, you cannot include that dependent in the calculation of this credit.*

Answer the following questions for each dependent listed on Form 1040, line 6c; Form 1040A, line 6c; or Form 1040NR, line 7c, who has an ITIN (Individual Taxpayer Identification Number) and that you indicated is a qualifying child for the child tax credit by checking column (4) for that dependent.

A For the first dependent identified with an ITIN and listed as a qualifying child for the child tax credit, did this child meet the substantial presence test? See separate instructions.

☑ Yes ☐ No

B For the second dependent identified with an ITIN and listed as a qualifying child for the child tax credit, did this child meet the substantial presence test? See separate instructions.

☑ Yes ☐ No

C For the third dependent identified with an ITIN and listed as a qualifying child for the child tax credit, did this child meet the substantial presence test? See separate instructions.

☐ Yes ☐ No

D For the fourth dependent identified with an ITIN and listed as a qualifying child for the child tax credit, did this child meet the substantial presence test? See separate instructions.

☐ Yes ☐ No

Note: If you have more than four dependents identified with an ITIN and listed as a qualifying child for the child tax credit, see separate instructions and check here . . . ▶ ☐

Part II — Additional Child Tax Credit Filers

1 If you file Form 2555 or 2555-EZ stop here; you cannot claim the additional child tax credit.

If you are required to use the worksheet in Pub. 972, enter the amount from line 8 of the Child Tax Credit Worksheet in the publication. Otherwise:

1040 filers: Enter the amount from line 6 of your Child Tax Credit Worksheet (see the Instructions for Form 1040, line 52).

1040A filers: Enter the amount from line 6 of your Child Tax Credit Worksheet (see the Instructions for Form 1040A, line 35).

1040NR filers: Enter the amount from line 6 of your Child Tax Credit Worksheet (see the Instructions for Form 1040NR, line 49). . . . **1** 2000 00

2 Enter the amount from Form 1040, line 52; Form 1040A, line 35; or Form 1040NR, line 49 . . . **2** 581 00

3 Subtract line 2 from line 1. If zero, stop here; you cannot claim this credit . . . **3** 1419 00

4a Earned income (see separate instructions) . . . **4a** 35271 00

b Nontaxable combat pay (see separate instructions) . . . **4b** 0

5 Is the amount on line 4a more than $3,000?

☐ No. Leave line 5 blank and enter -0- on line 6.

☑ Yes. Subtract $3,000 from the amount on line 4a. Enter the result . . . **5** 32271 00

6 Multiply the amount on line 5 by 15% (0.15) and enter the result . . . **6** 4841 00

Next. Do you have three or more qualifying children?

☑ No. If line 6 is zero, stop here; you cannot claim this credit. Otherwise, skip Part III and enter the smaller of line 3 or line 6 on line 13.

☐ Yes. If line 6 is equal to or more than line 3, skip Part III and enter the amount from line 3 on line 13. Otherwise, go to line 7.

For Paperwork Reduction Act Notice, see your tax return instructions. Cat. No. 59761M Schedule 8812 (Form 1040A or 1040) 2016

Schedule 8812 (Form 1040A or 1040) 2016 Page 2

Part III Certain Filers Who Have Three or More Qualifying Children

Line	Description		Box	Amount
7	Withheld social security, Medicare, and Additional Medicare taxes from Form(s) W-2, boxes 4 and 6. If married filing jointly, include your spouse's amounts with yours. If your employer withheld or you paid Additional Medicare Tax or tier 1 RRTA taxes, see separate instructions		7	
8	**1040 filers:**	Enter the total of the amounts from Form 1040, lines 27 and 58, plus any taxes that you identified using code "UT" and entered on line 62.		
	1040A filers:	Enter -0-.	8	
	1040NR filers:	Enter the total of the amounts from Form 1040NR, lines 27 and 56, plus any taxes that you identified using code "UT" and entered on line 60.		
9	Add lines 7 and 8		9	
10	**1040 filers:**	Enter the total of the amounts from Form 1040, lines 66a and 71.		
	1040A filers:	Enter the total of the amount from Form 1040A, line 42a, plus any excess social security and tier 1 RRTA taxes withheld that you entered to the left of line 46 (see separate instructions).	10	
	1040NR filers:	Enter the amount from Form 1040NR, line 67.		
11	Subtract line 10 from line 9. If zero or less, enter -0-		11	
12	Enter the larger of line 6 or line 11		12	
	Next, enter the smaller of line 3 or line 12 on line 13.			

Part IV Additional Child Tax Credit

13	This is your additional child tax credit	13	1419 00

1040 / 1040A / 1040NR ← Enter this amount on Form 1040, line 67, Form 1040A, line 43, or Form 1040NR, line 64.

Schedule 8812 (Form 1040A or 1040) 2016

Form **2441**

Department of the Treasury
Internal Revenue Service (99)

Child and Dependent Care Expenses

▶ Attach to Form 1040, Form 1040A, or Form 1040NR.

▶ Information about Form 2441 and its separate instructions is at *www.irs.gov/form2441.*

1040 / 1040A / 1040NR — 2441

OMB No. 1545-0074

2016

Attachment Sequence No. **21**

Name(s) shown on return: ■■ K. ■■ | Your social security number: ■■■

Part I **Persons or Organizations Who Provided the Care**—You must complete this part.
(If you have more than two care providers, see the instructions.)

1 (a) Care provider's name	(b) Address (number, street, apt. no., city, state, and ZIP code)	(c) Identifying number (SSN or EIN)	(d) Amount paid (see instructions)
KCAA Preschool of Hawaii	■■■ ■■■	GE 046-192-2304-01	3460 00

Did you receive dependent care benefits? — No ——▶ Complete only Part II below.
— Yes ——▶ Complete Part III on the back next.

Caution: If the care was provided in your home, you may owe employment taxes. If you do, you cannot file Form 1040A. For details, see the instructions for Form 1040, line 60a, or Form 1040NR, line 59a.

Part II **Credit for Child and Dependent Care Expenses**

2 Information about your qualifying person(s). If you have more than two qualifying persons, see the instructions.

(a) Qualifying person's name — First	Last	(b) Qualifying person's social security number	(c) Qualified expenses you incurred and paid in 2016 for the person listed in column (a)
■■	■■	■■■	3460 00

3	Add the amounts in column (c) of line 2. Do not enter more than $3,000 for one qualifying person or $6,000 for two or more persons. If you completed Part III, enter the amount from line 31	3	3000 00
4	Enter your earned income. See instructions	4	35271 00
5	If married filing jointly, enter your spouse's earned income (if you or your spouse was a student or was disabled, see the instructions); all others, enter the amount from line 4	5	35271 00
6	Enter the smallest of line 3, 4, or 5	6	3000 00
7	Enter the amount from Form 1040, line 38; Form 1040A, line 22; or Form 1040NR, line 37	7	
8	Enter on line 8 the decimal amount shown below that applies to the amount on line 7	8	X. 24

If line 7 is: Over	But not over	Decimal amount is	If line 7 is: Over	But not over	Decimal amount is
$0	15,000	.35	$29,000	31,000	.27
15,000	17,000	.34	31,000	33,000	.26
17,000	19,000	.33	33,000	35,000	.25
19,000	21,000	.32	35,000	37,000	.24
21,000	23,000	.31	37,000	39,000	.23
23,000	25,000	.30	39,000	41,000	.22
25,000	27,000	.29	41,000	43,000	.21
27,000	29,000	.28	43,000	No limit	.20

9	Multiply line 6 by the decimal amount on line 8. If you paid 2015 expenses in 2016, see the instructions	9	720 00
10	Tax liability limit. Enter the amount from the Credit Limit Worksheet in the instructions	10	
11	**Credit for child and dependent care expenses.** Enter the smaller of line 9 or line 10 here and on Form 1040, line 49; Form 1040A, line 31; or Form 1040NR, line 47	11	720 00

For Paperwork Reduction Act Notice, see your tax return instructions. Cat. No. 11862M Form **2441** (2016)

EXHIBIT '11':
Petitioner's 2016 Tax Return with W-2 Form

ROSETTA STONE *ASSOCIATES IN TRANSLATION*

7375 N. Calle sin Celo, Tucson, AZ 85718 • (520) 575-9200 • rosettrans@aol.com • www.rosettrans.com
• ATACertified •

Certification

AT THE REQUEST OF THE INTERESTED PARTY, I hereby certify that I have translated the following document:

Certificate of Absence of Criminal History
concerning [redacted]

from the Spanish into the English language on this 27th day of September 2017, and that the information contained in the translated document is a true, complete and correct reflection of the original text, to the best of my ability as a Professional Translator.

ROSETTA STONE ASSOCIATES IN TRANSLATION

Carola P. Myers

CAROLA P. MYERS
Member, A.C.I.A. - ATA-Certified

Your Dependable Source of Foreign Language Translation and Interpretation

Translation from Spanish
27 September 2017

[Initials]

The Free and Sovereign State of Hidalgo

Office of the Attorney General

The State of Hidalgo grows with you

Directorate General of Expert Services
Department of Personal Identification

1359
No. 57699 B

TO WHOM IT MAY CONCERN:
THE DIRECTOR GENERAL OF EXPERT SERVICES OF THE OFFICE OF THE ATTORNEY GENERAL OF THE FREE AND SOVEREIGN STATE OF HIDALGO,

Certifies:

[Signature]
Signature of Interested Party

That, a thorough search of the alphabetic and fingerprint archives of the Department of Personal Identification and of the National Registry of Fingerprints having been conducted, **NO** record of any criminal history of

whose photograph, signature, and impression of the right index finger appear in the median upper margin, has been found.

This **CERTIFICATE** is being issued at the request of the interested party for any legal purposes and subject to compliance with the requirements for the exclusive purpose of:

ISSUANCE OF VISA

Issued at the City of Pachuca de Soto, Hidalgo, on this 5th day of SEPTEMBER, 2017.

SINCERELY,

[Signature]
SUSANA PELÁEZ LARA
DIRECTOR GENERAL OF EXPERT SERVICES

Folio 57699-B
Payment 8747568
Recorded by CELIA

IMPORTANT: THIS CERTIFICATE IS VALID FOR THIRTY DAYS FROM DATE OF ISSUANCE. ANY ALTERATIONS RENDER THIS DOCUMENT INVALID.
*Pursuant to the provisions of Articles 16, 18, 19 and 20 of the Constitution of the United Mexican States. Articles 3, 9 and 11 Section V, 12 and 14, Sections I, III, XXXI of the Charter of the Attorney General's Office. Articles 1, 3, 5 and 8, Subsection C, Sections LXII, 19, 105 and 106, Section XV; as well as the provisions of Decree A/023/12 of the Federal Attorney General's Office governing the issuance of registration data and the procedure for canceling or returning registration data; as well as to provide information, certificates or certifications pertaining thereto; published in the Official Gazette of the Federation on 09 (nine) February, 2012 (two thousand and twelve).

Rosetta Stone Translations • Tucson, Arizona
(520) 575-9200 • rosettrans@aol.com • www.rosettrans.com

Procuraduría General de Justicia
Hidalgo crece contigo

Estado Libre y Soberano de Hidalgo

Dirección General de Servicios Periciales
Departamento de Identificación Humana

1359
Nº 57699 B

A QUIEN CORRESPONDA:
EL C. DIRECTOR GENERAL DE SERVICIOS PERICIALES DE LA PROCURADURÍA GENERAL DE JUSTICIA DEL ESTADO LIBRE Y SOBERANO DE HIDALGO,

Hace constar que:

Firma del interesado(a)

Que habiéndose realizado minuciosa búsqueda en los archivos alfabéticos y dactiloscópicos del Gabinete de Identificación Humana, así como en el Registro Nacional de Huellas Dactilares, **NO** se encontró registro de antecedentes penales del (la) C.

Cuya fotografía, firma e impresión dactilar del dedo índice derecho obran al margen medio superior.

Se expide la presente **CONSTANCIA** a solicitud del (la) interesado(a) para los usos legales y previo el cumplimiento de los requisitos exigidos para el trámite exclusivo de:

TRÁMITE VISA

En la ciudad de Pachuca de Soto, Hidalgo, a los 5 días del mes de SEPTIEMBRE del año 2017.

ATENTAMENTE

EXHIBIT '12':
Online DS-260 Application

U.S. DEPARTMENT of STATE
CONSULAR ELECTRONIC APPLICATION CENTER

Online Immigrant Visa and Alien Registration Application (DS-260)

OMB NUMBER: 1405-0185
FORM NUMBER: DS-260
EXPIRATION DATE: 04/30/2019
ESTIMATED BURDEN: 120 MIN

Personal Information 1

NOTE: Data on this page must match the information as it is written in your passport or travel documents.

Surnames

(e.g., FERNANDEZ GARCIA)

Help: Surnames

Enter all surnames as listed in your passport or travel documentation. If only one name is listed, enter that as your surname.

Given Names

(e.g., JUAN MIGUEL)

Full Name in Native Alphabet

☑ Does Not Apply/Technology Not Available

Help: Given Names

Your given name includes any first name and any middle name that is listed in your passport or travel documentation. If your passport or travel documentation does not include a given name, please enter 'FNU' in Given Names.

Have you ever used other names (i.e., maiden, religious, professional, alias, etc.)?

○ Yes ◉ No

Help: Other Names Used

Other names used includes your maiden name, religious name, professional name, or any other names by which you are known or have been known in the past.

Sex

◉ Male ○ Female

Current Marital Status

MARRIED

Date of Birth

24 ▾ FEB ▾ 1980
(Format: DD-MMM-YYYY)

City of Birth

TEPEPA ACAXOCHITLAN

State/Province of Birth

HIDALGO

Does Not Apply

Country/Region of Birth

MEXICO - HIDALGO

Help: Date of Birth

If day or month is unknown, enter as shown in passport or travel document.

Help: Country/Region of Birth

The name of the country/region should be the name that is currently in use for the place where you were born.

PAPERWORK REDUCTION ACT: Public reporting burden for this collection of information is estimated to average 120 minutes per response, including time required for searching existing data sources, gathering the necessary documentation, providing the information and/or documents required, and reviewing the final collection. You do not have to supply this information unless this collection displays a currently valid OMB control number. If you have comments on the accuracy of this burden estimate and/or recommendations for reducing it, please send them to: **PRA_BurdenComments@state.gov**

CONFIDENTIALITY STATEMENT: AUTHORITIES: The information asked for on this form is requested pursuant to Section 222 of the Immigration and Nationality Act. Section 222(f) provides that the records of the Department of State and of diplomatic and consular offices of the United States pertaining to the issuance and refusal of visas or permits to enter the United States shall be considered confidential and shall be used only for the formulation, amendment, administration, or enforcement of the immigration, nationality, and other laws of the United States. Certified copies of such records may be made available to a court provided the court certifies that the information contained in such records is needed in a case pending before the court. PURPOSE: The U.S. Department of State uses the facts you provide on this form primarily to determine your classification and eligibility for a U.S. immigrant visa. Individuals who fail to submit this form or who do not provide all the requested information may be denied a U.S. immigrant visa. Although furnishing this information is voluntary, failure to provide this information may delay or prevent the processing of your case. ROUTINE USES: If you are issued an immigrant visa and are subsequently admitted to the United States as an immigrant, the Department of Homeland Security will use the information on this form to issue you a Permanent Resident Card, and, if you so indicate, the Social Security Administration will use the information to issue a social security number. The information provided may also be released to federal agencies for law enforcement, counterterrorism and homeland security purposes; to Congress and courts within their sphere of jurisdiction; and to other federal agencies who may need the information to administer or enforce U.S. laws.

Back: Getting Started Save Next: Personal 2

U.S. DEPARTMENT of STATE
CONSULAR ELECTRONIC APPLICATION CENTER

Online Immigrant Visa and Alien Registration Application (DS-260)

Personal Information 2

Country/Region of Origin (Nationality)

MEXICO ▼

Provide the following information on your travel documentation:

Document Type

PASSPORT ▼

Document ID

Q17188218

Country/Authority that Issued Document

MEXICO ▼

Issuance Date	Expiration Date
29 ▼ MAY ▼ 2015	29 ▼ MAY ▼ 2021
(Format: DD-MMM-YYYY)	(Format: DD-MMM-YYYY)

Help: Travel Documentation

Enter the information on the travel document you will be using when traveling to the U.S. Your travel document should be a valid, unexpired passport or other valid, unexpired documentation that is sufficient to establish your identity and nationality.

Do you hold or have you held any nationality other than the one you have indicated above?

○ Yes ◉ No

Help: Other Country/Region of Origin (Nationality)

Enter all nationalities you currently hold and all nationalities you have previously held, regardless of whether you have formally and/or legally relinquished the nationality. If the country where you previously held nationality is no longer a political entity or country, select the nationality that corresponds with the name of the country that is currently used for that location.

U.S. DEPARTMENT of STATE
CONSULAR ELECTRONIC APPLICATION CENTER

Online Immigrant Visa and Alien Registration Application (DS-260)

Present and Previous Address Information

Present Address

Street Address (Line 1)

Street Address (Line 2)
*Optional

City

TULACINGO

State/Province

HIDALGO
☐ Does Not Apply

Postal Zone/ZIP Code

☑ Does Not Apply

Country/Region

MEXICO

Started Living Here
JUN 2005
(Format: MMM-YYYY)

Previous Addresses

Have you lived anywhere other than this address since the age of sixteen? (Date you turned sixteen: 24-Feb-1996)

(•) Yes ( ) No

Please provide the following information on all addresses you lived at since turning sixteen. Begin with your address **immediately before** your current address.

Street Address (Line 1)

HOKUMAHOE ST.

Street Address (Line 2)
*Optional

Help: Previous Addresses

Previous addresses should only include those addresses at which you established a residence (for example on campus housing where you lived for an academic term at your college or university) and should not include places at which you were temporarily present (for example a hotel at which you stayed for vacation).

City

LAUPAHOEHOE

State/Province

HAWAII

☐ Does Not Apply

Postal Zone/ZIP Code

96764

☐ Does Not Apply

Country/Region

UNITED STATES OF AMERICA ▼

Started Living Here

FEB ▼ 2004

(Format: MMM-YYYY)

To Date

JUN ▼ 2005

(Format: MMM-YYYY)

Add Another Remove

Street Address (Line 1)

Street Address (Line 2)

Optional

BAR HUITZILINGO

City

ACAXOCHITLAN

State/Province

HIDALGO

☐ Does Not Apply

Postal Zone/ZIP Code

43730

☐ Does Not Apply

Country/Region

MEXICO ▼

Started Living Here

MAR ▼ 2003

(Format: MMM-YYYY)

To Date

(Format: MMM-YYYY)

Add Another Remove

Street Address (Line 1)

HOKUMAHOE ST.

Street Address (Line 2)
Optional

City

LAUPAHOEHOE

State/Province

HAWAII
Does Not Apply

Postal Zone/ZIP Code

96764
Does Not Apply

Country/Region

UNITED STATES OF AMERICA

Started Living Here
APR 2001
(Format: MMM-YYYY)

To Date
MAR 2003
(Format: MMM-YYYY)

Add Another Remove

Street Address (Line 1)

LOC PAREDONES S N

Street Address (Line 2)
Optional
BARR HUITZILINGO

City

ACAXOCHITLAN

State/Province

HIDALGO
Does Not Apply

Postal Zone/ZIP Code

43730

Does Not Apply

Country/Region

MEXICO

Started Living Here

FEB 1996

(Format: MMM-YYYY)

To Date

APR 2001

(Format: MMM-YYYY)

Add Another Remove

Phone

Primary Phone Number

Secondary Phone Number

Does Not Apply

Work Phone Number

Does Not Apply

Email

Email Address

(e.g., emailaddress@example.com)

Help: Email

You must provide an email address. The email address you provide will be used for correspondence purposes. Provide an email address that is secure and to which you have reasonable access.

Back: Personal Save Next: Mailing/Permanent

Online Immigrant Visa and Alien Registration Application (DS-260)

Mailing and Permanent Address Information

Mailing Address

Is your Mailing Address the same as your Present Address?

( ) Yes (•) No

Complete the additional items below:

Address (Line 1)

LISTA DE CORREOS

Address (Line 2)
*Optional

City

TULANCINGO

State/Province

HIDALGO

[ ] Does Not Apply

Postal Zone/ZIP Code

43600

[ ] Does Not Apply

Country/Region

MEXICO

Help: Mailing Address

This is the address where we will send correspondence regarding your application.

Permanent Address

Please provide the following information on where you intend to live after arrival in the United States.

Name of person currently living at address

[ ] Does Not Apply

U.S. Street Address (Line 1)

*Optional

City

HONOLULU

State

HAWAII

ZIP Code

96819

(e.g., 12345 or 12345-1234)

Phone Number

(e.g., 555-555-5555)

Does Not Apply

Is this address where you want your Permanent Residence Card (Green Card) mailed?

Yes No

Back: Present/Previous Save Next: Family

U.S. DEPARTMENT of STATE
CONSULAR ELECTRONIC APPLICATION CENTER

Online Immigrant Visa and Alien Registration Application (DS-260)

Family Information: Parents

NOTE: Please provide the following information concerning your biological parents. If you are adopted, please provide the following information on your adoptive parents.

Father

Surnames
(e.g., Hernandez Garcia)
☐ Do Not Know

Given Names
(e.g., Juan Miguel)
☐ Do Not Know

Date of Birth
20 DEC 1951
(Format: DD-MMM-YYYY) ☐ Do Not Know

Place of Birth

City
☐ Do Not Know

State/Province

☑ Do Not Know

Country/Region
MEXICO - HIDALGO
☐ Do Not Know

Is your father still living?

○ Yes ● No

Year of Death
1988

Mother

Surnames at Birth

(e.g., Hernandez Garcia)

Do Not Know

Given Names

(e.g., Juanita Miguel)

Do Not Know

Date of Birth

24 APR 1962

(Format: DD-MMM-YYYY) Do Not Know

Place of Birth

City

Do Not Know

State/Province

Do Not Know

Country/Region

MEXICO - HIDALGO

Do Not Know

Is your mother still living?

Yes No

Is your mother's address the same as your father's?

Yes No

Current Address

Do Not Know

Street Address (Line 1)

Street Address (Line 2)

Optional

City

TULACINGO

State/Province

Does Not Apply

Postal Zone/ZIP Code

43633

Does Not Apply

Country/Region

MEXICO

Back: Address and Phone Save Next: Spouse

U.S. DEPARTMENT of STATE
CONSULAR ELECTRONIC APPLICATION CENTER

Online Immigrant Visa and Alien Registration Application (DS-260)

Family Information: Spouse

NOTE: Please provide the following information on your current spouse.

Current Spouse

Surnames

Given Names

Date of Birth
22 ▼ JAN ▼ 1976
(Format: DD-MMM-YYYY)

Place of Birth

City
HONOLULU

☐ Do Not Know

State/Province of Birth
HAWAII

☐ Does Not Apply

Country/Region
UNITED STATES OF AMERICA ▼

Spouse's Address

SAME AS INTENDED U.S. ADDRESS ▼

Occupation

OTHER ▼

Provide the following information:

Specify Other

FINANCIAL SERVICE REPRESENTATIVE

Date and Place of Marriage

Date of Marriage
28 ▼ JUL ▼ 2005
(Format: DD-MMM-YYYY)

City

State/Province
HIDALGO ☐
Does Not Apply

Country/Region
MEXICO ▼

Is your spouse immigrating to the U.S. with you?

○ ◉
Yes No

Is your spouse immigrating to the U.S. at a later date to join you?

○ ◉
Yes No

Back: Parents Save Next: Previous Spouse

U.S. DEPARTMENT of STATE
CONSULAR ELECTRONIC APPLICATION CENTER

Online Immigrant Visa and Alien Registration Application (DS-260)

Family Information: Previous Spouse

NOTE: Please provide the following information on all of your previous spouses, including those deceased.

Do you have any previous spouses?

Yes No

Back: Spouse   Save   Next: Children

U.S. DEPARTMENT of STATE
CONSULAR ELECTRONIC APPLICATION CENTER

Online Immigrant Visa and Alien Registration Application (DS-260)

Family Information: Children

NOTE: The Immigration and Nationality Act (INA) does not allow derivative status to family members of immediate relatives. For example, IR1, CR1, IR2, CR2 and IR5 classifications are immediate relative visa categories. The petitioner must file separate immediate relative petitions for the spouse, each child and each parent.

Do you have any children?

(•) Yes ( ) No

Number of Children: 2

Provide the following information on each of your children (this includes all natural children, adopted children, and step children).

Child 1

Surnames

Given Names

Date of Birth

01 ▾ MAR ▾ 2005

(Format: DD-MMM-YYYY)

Place of Birth

City

☐ Do Not Know

State/Province

HAWAII ☐ Does Not Apply

Country/Region

UNITED STATES OF AMERICA ▾

Does this child live with you?

( ) Yes (•) No

Help: Children Information

The Immigration and Nationality Act (INA) does not allow derivative status for family members of immediate relatives. IR1, CR1, IR2, CR2 and IR5 classifications are immediate relative visa categories. If you have questions about whether or not your child is allowed to immigrate to the U.S. with you or is allowed to follow to join in the U.S., please see travel.state.gov for more information.

Do Not Know

Street Address (Line 1)

Street Address (Line 2)
Optional

City

HONOLULU

State/Province

HAWAII
Does Not Apply

Postal Zone/ZIP Code

96819
Does Not Apply

Country/Region

UNITED STATES OF AMERICA

Is this child immigrating to the U.S. with you?

Yes No

Is this child immigrating to the U.S. at a later date to join you?

Yes No

Add Another Remove

Child 2

Surnames

Given Names

Date of Birth
09 OCT 2012
(Format: DD-MMM-YYYY)

Place of Birth

City
HONOLULU

Do Not Know

State/Province

HAWAII

Does Not Apply

Country/Region

UNITED STATES OF AMERICA

Does this child live with you?

Yes No

Address

Do Not Know

Street Address (Line 1)

Street Address (Line 2)

Optional

City

HONOLULU

State/Province

HAWAII

Does Not Apply

Postal Zone/ZIP Code

96819

Does Not Apply

Country/Region

UNITED STATES OF AMERICA

Is this child immigrating to the U.S. with you?

Yes No

Is this child immigrating to the U.S. at a later date to join you?

Yes No

Add Another Remove

U.S. DEPARTMENT of STATE
CONSULAR ELECTRONIC APPLICATION CENTER

Online Immigrant Visa and Alien Registration Application (DS-260)

Previous U.S. Travel Information

NOTE: Provide the following previous U.S. travel information. Provide complete and accurate information to all questions that require an explanation.

Have you ever been in the U.S.?

(•) Yes ( ) No

Provide the following information:

Were you issued an Alien Registration Number by the Department of Homeland Security?

( ) Yes (•) No

Provide information on your last five U.S. visits:

Date Arrived
01 ▼ APR ▼ 2001
(Format: DD-MMM-YYYY)

Length of Stay
2 YEAR(S) ▼

Add Another Remove

Date Arrived
01 ▼ APR ▼ 2004
(Format: DD-MMM-YYYY)

Length of Stay
1 YEAR(S) ▼

Add Another Remove

Help: Previous U.S. Visits

If you are unsure about when you visited the U.S., please provide a best estimate.

Have you ever been issued a U.S. Visa?

( ) Yes (•) No

Have you ever been refused a U.S. Visa, been refused admission to the United States, or withdrawn your application for admission at the port of entry?

Yes No

Explain

IN 2004, I ENTERED EWI AND WAS RETURNED

Back: Family Save Next: Work / Education / Training

U.S. DEPARTMENT of STATE
CONSULAR ELECTRONIC APPLICATION CENTER

Online Immigrant Visa and Alien Registration Application (DS-260)

Present Work/Education/Training Information

NOTE: Provide the following information concerning your current employment or education.

Primary Occupation

OTHER

Provide the following information:

Specify Other

CONSTRUCTION

Present Employer or School Name

SELF EMPLOYED

Present Employer or School address:

Street Address (Line 1)

209 CALLE CEDROS COL. VIVEROS DE LA LOMA

Street Address (Line 2) *Optional

State/Province

HIDALGO

Does Not Apply

Postal Zone/ZIP Code

Does Not Apply

Country/Region

MEXICO

Do you have other occupations?

○ ◉
Yes No

In which occupation do you intend to work in the U.S.?

OTHER ▼

Provide the following information:

Specify Other

CONSTRUCTION

Back: Previous U.S. Travel Save Next: Work/Education: Previous

U.S. DEPARTMENT of STATE
CONSULAR ELECTRONIC APPLICATION CENTER

Online Immigrant Visa and Alien Registration Application (DS-260)

Previous Work/Education/Training Information

NOTE: Please provide the following information.

Were you previously employed?

Yes No

Have you attended any educational institutions at a secondary level or above?

Yes No

Help: Level of Education

You must answer yes to this question if you have ever attended high school, college, university, graduate school, doctoral program, or a vocational program.

Back: Work/Education: Present   Save   Next: Work/Education: Additional

U.S. DEPARTMENT of STATE
CONSULAR ELECTRONIC APPLICATION CENTER

Online Immigrant Visa and Alien Registration Application (DS-260)

Additional Work/Education/Training Information

NOTE: Provide the following work, education, or training related information. Provide complete and accurate information to all questions that require an explanation.

Have you ever served in the military?

Yes No

Have you belonged to, contributed to, or worked for any professional, social, or charitable organization?

Yes No

Do you have any specialized skills or training, such as firearms, explosives, nuclear, biological, or chemical experience?

Yes No

Have you ever served in, been a member of, or been involved with a paramilitary unit, vigilante unit, rebel group, guerrilla group, or insurgent organization?

Yes No

Can you speak and/or read languages other than your native language?

Yes No

U.S. DEPARTMENT of STATE
CONSULAR ELECTRONIC APPLICATION CENTER

Online Immigrant Visa and Alien Registration Application (DS-260)

Petitioner Information

NOTE: Please provide the following information concerning the individual/entity that filed a petition on your behalf.

Petitioner is my
SPOUSE

Petitioner

Petitioner Surnames
RIOS

Petitioner Given Names
CHELSIE KIYOMI NALANI

Address and Phone Number of Petitioner

Street Address (Line 1)
1808 MANIKI PLACE

Street Address (Line 2) *Optional*

City
HONOLULU

State/Province
HAWAII
Does Not Apply

Postal Zone/ZIP Code
96819
Does Not Apply

Country/Region
UNITED STATES OF AMERICA

Telephone
(808)225-5279
(e.g., 555-555-5555)

Mobile/Cell Telephone
(808)225-5279
Does Not Apply
(e.g., 555-555-5555)

Email Address

Help: Petitioner

Your petitioner is generally the U.S. person or business who made a formal request that you be considered for an immigrant visa or permanent legal residence. Your petitioner is generally your U.S. citizen relative, your U.S. permanent resident relative, or your U.S. employer. In some cases you may have filed a petition on your own behalf.

Help: Email Address

The email address you provide for the petitioner may be used for correspondence purposes. Please provide an email address that is secure and to which your petitioner has reasonable access.

(e.g., emailaddress@example.com)

Back: Work / Education / Training   Save   Next: Security and Background

U.S. DEPARTMENT of STATE
CONSULAR ELECTRONIC APPLICATION CENTER

Online Immigrant Visa and Alien Registration Application (DS-260)

Security and Background: Medical and Health Information

NOTE: Provide the following security and background information. Provide complete and accurate information to all questions that require an explanation. A visa may not be issued to persons who are within specific categories defined by law as inadmissible to the United States (except when a waiver is obtained in advance). Are any of the following applicable to you? A YES answer does not automatically signify ineligibility for a visa. **Please note that should you answer Yes to any of the following questions, you may be requested to provide documentation to support your explanation.**

Do you have a communicable disease of public health significance such as tuberculosis (TB)?

○ ◉
Yes No

Do you have documentation to establish that you have received vaccinations in accordance with U.S. law?

◉ ○
Yes No

Do you have a mental or physical disorder that poses or is likely to pose a threat to the safety or welfare of yourself or others?

○ ◉
Yes No

Are you or have you ever been a drug abuser or addict?

○ ◉
Yes No

Back: Petitioner Save Next: Criminal

U.S. DEPARTMENT of STATE
CONSULAR ELECTRONIC APPLICATION CENTER

Online Immigrant Visa and Alien Registration Application (DS-260)

Security and Background: Criminal Information

NOTE: Provide the following security and background information. Provide complete and accurate information to all questions that require an explanation. A visa may not be issued to persons who are within specific categories defined by law as inadmissible to the United States (except when a waiver is obtained in advance). Are any of the following applicable to you? A YES answer does not automatically signify ineligibility for a visa. **Please note that should you answer Yes to any of the following questions, you may be requested to provide documentation to support your explanation.**

Have you ever been arrested or convicted for any offense or crime, even though subject of a pardon, amnesty, or other similar action?

Yes No

Have you ever violated, or engaged in a conspiracy to violate, any law relating to controlled substances?

Yes No

Are you the spouse, son, or daughter of an individual who has violated any controlled substance trafficking law, and have knowingly benefited from the trafficking activities in the past five years?

Yes No

Are you coming to the United States to engage in prostitution or unlawful commercialized vice or have you been engaged in prostitution or procuring prostitutes within the past 10 years?

Yes No

Have you ever been involved in, or do you seek to engage in, money laundering?

Have you ever committed or conspired to commit a human trafficking offense in the United States or outside the United States?

○ ◉
Yes No

Have you ever knowingly aided, abetted, assisted, or colluded with an individual who has been identified by the President of the United States as a person who plays a significant role in a severe form of trafficking in persons?

○ ◉
Yes No

Are you the spouse, son, or daughter of an individual who has committed or conspired to commit a human trafficking offense in the United States or outside the United States and have you within the last five years, knowingly benefited from the trafficking activities?

○ ◉
Yes No

Back: Medical and Health   Save   Next: Security 1

U.S. DEPARTMENT of STATE
CONSULAR ELECTRONIC APPLICATION CENTER

Online Immigrant Visa and Alien Registration Application (DS-260)

Security and Background: Security Information 1

NOTE: Provide the following security and background information. Provide complete and accurate information to all questions that require an explanation. A visa may not be issued to persons who are within specific categories defined by law as inadmissible to the United States (except when a waiver is obtained in advance). Are any of the following applicable to you? A YES answer does not automatically signify ineligibility for a visa. **Please note that should you answer Yes to any of the following questions, you may be requested to provide documentation to support your explanation.**

Do you seek to engage in espionage, sabotage, export control violations, or any other illegal activity while in the United States?

○ ◉
Yes No

Do you seek to engage in terrorist activities while in the United States or have you ever engaged in terrorist activities?

○ ◉
Yes No

Have you ever or do you intend to provide financial assistance or other support to terrorists or terrorist organizations?

○ ◉
Yes No

Are you a member or representative of a terrorist organization?

○ ◉
Yes No

Have you ever ordered, incited, committed, assisted, or otherwise participated in genocide?

○ ◉
Yes No

U.S. DEPARTMENT of STATE

CONSULAR ELECTRONIC APPLICATION CENTER

Online Immigrant Visa and Alien Registration Application (DS-260)

Security and Background: Security Information 2

NOTE: Provide the following security and background information. Provide complete and accurate information to all questions that require an explanation. A visa may not be issued to persons who are within specific categories defined by law as inadmissible to the United States (except when a waiver is obtained in advance). Are any of the following applicable to you? A YES answer does not automatically signify ineligibility for a visa. **Please note that should you answer Yes to any of the following questions, you may be requested to provide documentation to support your explanation.**

Are you a member of or affiliated with the Communist or other totalitarian party?

Yes No

Have you ever directly or indirectly assisted or supported any of the groups in Colombia known as the Revolutionary Armed Forces of Colombia (FARC), National Liberation Army (ELN), or United Self-Defense Forces of Colombia (AUC)?

Yes No

Have you ever, through abuse of governmental or political position converted for personal gain, confiscated or expropriated property in a foreign nation to which a United States national had claim of ownership?

Yes No

Are you the spouse, minor child, or agent of an individual who has through abuse of governmental or political position converted for personal gain, confiscated or expropriated property in a foreign nation to which a United States national had claim of ownership?

Yes No

Have you ever been directly involved in the establishment or enforcement of population controls forcing a woman to undergo an abortion against her free choice or a man or a

Yes No

Have you ever disclosed or trafficked in confidential U.S. business information obtained in connection with U.S. participation in the Chemical Weapons Convention?

Yes No

Are you the spouse, minor child, or agent of an individual who has disclosed or trafficked in confidential U.S. business information obtained in connection with U.S. participation in the Chemical Weapons Convention?

Yes No

Back: Security 1 Save Next: Immig. Law Violations 1

U.S. DEPARTMENT of STATE
CONSULAR ELECTRONIC APPLICATION CENTER

Online Immigrant Visa and Alien Registration Application (DS-260)

Security and Background: Immigration Law Violations Information 1

NOTE: Provide the following security and background information. Provide complete and accurate information to all questions that require an explanation. A visa may not be issued to persons who are within specific categories defined by law as inadmissible to the United States (except when a waiver is obtained in advance). Are any of the following applicable to you? A YES answer does not automatically signify ineligibility for a visa. **Please note that should you answer Yes to any of the following questions, you may be requested to provide documentation to support your explanation.**

Have you ever sought to obtain or assist others to obtain a visa, entry into the United States, or any other United States immigration benefit by fraud or willful misrepresentation or other unlawful means?

(●) Yes ( ) No

Explain

IN 2004, I CROSSED THE BORDER IN ARIZONA UNDOCUMENTED BUT WAS CAUGHT BY US BORDER PATROL. THIS ILLEGAL CROSSING WAS DOCUMENTED AND THE US IMMIGRATION HAS A RECORD OF IT.

Have you ever been the subject of a removal or deportation hearing?

( ) Yes (●) No

Have you failed to attend a hearing on removability or inadmissibility within the last five years?

( ) Yes (●) No

Have you ever been unlawfully present, overstayed the amount of time granted by an immigration official or otherwise violated the terms of a U.S. visa?

( ) Yes (●) No

Are you subject to a civil penalty under INA 274C?

Yes No

Have you been ordered removed from the U.S. during the last five years?

Yes No

Have you been ordered removed from the U.S. for a second time within the last 20 years?

Yes No

Back: Security 2 Save Next: Immig. Law Violations 2

U.S. DEPARTMENT of STATE
CONSULAR ELECTRONIC APPLICATION CENTER

Online Immigrant Visa and Alien Registration Application (DS-260)

Security and Background: Immigration Law Violations Information 2

NOTE: Provide the following security and background information. Provide complete and accurate information to all questions that require an explanation. A visa may not be issued to persons who are within specific categories defined by law as inadmissible to the United States (except when a waiver is obtained in advance). Are any of the following applicable to you? A YES answer does not automatically signify ineligibility for a visa. **Please note that should you answer Yes to any of the following questions, you may be requested to provide documentation to support your explanation.**

Have you ever been unlawfully present and ordered removed from the U.S. during the last ten years?

Yes No

Have you ever been convicted of an aggravated felony and been ordered removed from the U.S.?

Yes No

Have you ever been unlawfully present in the U.S. for more than 180 days (but no more than one year) and have voluntarily departed the U.S. within the last three years?

Yes No

Have you ever been unlawfully present in the U.S. for more than one year or more than one year in the aggregate at any time during the last 10 years?

Yes No

Back: Immig. Law Violations 1 Save Next: Miscellaneous 1

U.S. DEPARTMENT of STATE
CONSULAR ELECTRONIC APPLICATION CENTER

Online Immigrant Visa and Alien Registration Application (DS-260)

Security and Background: Miscellaneous Information 1

NOTE: Provide the following security and background information. Provide complete and accurate information to all questions that require an explanation. A visa may not be issued to persons who are within specific categories defined by law as inadmissible to the United States (except when a waiver is obtained in advance). Are any of the following applicable to you? A YES answer does not automatically signify ineligibility for a visa. **Please note that should you answer Yes to any of the following questions, you may be requested to provide documentation to support your explanation.**

Have you ever withheld custody of a U.S. citizen child outside the United States from a person granted legal custody by a U.S. court?

Yes No

Have you ever intentionally assisted another person in withholding custody of a U.S. citizen child outside the United States from a person granted legal custody by a U.S. court?

Yes No

Have you voted in the United States in violation of any law or regulation?

Yes No

Have you ever renounced United States citizenship for the purpose of avoiding taxation?

Yes No

Have you attended a public elementary school or a public secondary school on student (F) status after November 30, 1996 without reimbursing the school?

Yes No

Do you seek to enter the United States for the purpose of performing skilled or unskilled labor but have not yet been certified by the Secretary of Labor?

Yes No

Are you a graduate of a foreign medical school seeking to perform medical services in the United States but have not yet passed the National Board of Medical Examiners examination or its equivalent?

Yes No

Back: Immig. Law Violations 2 Save Next: Miscellaneous 2

U.S. DEPARTMENT of STATE
CONSULAR ELECTRONIC APPLICATION CENTER

Online Immigrant Visa and Alien Registration Application (DS-260)

Security and Background: Miscellaneous Information 2

NOTE: Provide the following security and background information. Provide complete and accurate information to all questions that require an explanation. A visa may not be issued to persons who are within specific categories defined by law as inadmissible to the United States (except when a waiver is obtained in advance). Are any of the following applicable to you? A YES answer does not automatically signify ineligibility for a visa. **Please note that should you answer Yes to any of the following questions, you may be requested to provide documentation to support your explanation.**

Are you a health care worker seeking to perform such work in the United States but have not yet received certification from the Commission on Graduates of Foreign Nursing Schools or from an equivalent approved independent credentialing organization?

Yes No

Are you permanently ineligible for U.S. citizenship?

Yes No

Have you ever departed the United States in order to evade military service during a time of war?

Yes No

Are you coming to the U.S. to practice polygamy?

Yes No

Are you a former exchange visitor (J) who has not yet fulfilled the two-year foreign residence requirement?

Yes No

Has the Secretary of Homeland Security of the United States ever determined that you knowingly made a frivolous application for asylum?

Yes No

Are you likely to become a public charge after you are admitted to the United States?

Yes No

Back: Miscellaneous 1 Save Next: Social Security Number

U.S. DEPARTMENT of STATE
CONSULAR ELECTRONIC APPLICATION CENTER

Online Immigrant Visa and Alien Registration Application (DS-260)

Social Security Number Information

NOTE: Provide the following Social Security Number information. Provide complete and accurate information to all questions that require an explanation.

Have you ever applied for a Social Security number?

○ Yes ◉ No

Help: Social Security Number

A Social Security Number is a nine-digit number issued to U.S. citizens, permanent residents, and temporary residents present in the U.S. for the purpose of employment and is issued by the Social Security Administration.

Do you authorize disclosure of information from this form to the Department of Homeland Security, the Social Security Administration, and such other U.S. Government agencies as may be required for the purposes of assigning you a social security number (SSN) and issuing you a Social Security card and do you authorize the Social Security Administration to share your SSN with the Department of Homeland Security?

◉ Yes ○ No

If you answer 'No' to this question you will not receive a social security card.

Help: Consent to Disclosure

The applicant's response does not limit or restrict the Government's ability to obtain his or her social security number or other information on this form for enforcement or other purposes as authorized by law.

Back: Security and Background | Save | Next: Review

U.S. DEPARTMENT of STATE
CONSULAR ELECTRONIC APPLICATION CENTER

Online Immigrant Visa and Alien Registration Application (DS-260)

Personal, Address, and Phone Information

Note: You have completed data entry for your 'Immigrant Visa and Alien Registration' application. Before submitting the application, please review your entries below. To navigate to the next section to be reviewed, click the 'Next' button on the bottom of the page. If an entry is incorrect, click on the links on the right side of the page, which will direct you to the page where you entered the data. Once you have reviewed all sections, you will be directed to the Sign and Submit page to complete the application process.

Name Provided:	[redacted] , [redacted]
Full Name in Native Language:	DOES NOT APPLY/TECHNOLOGY NOT AVAILABLE
Other Names Used:	NO
Sex:	MALE
Current Marital Status:	MARRIED
Date of Birth:	24 FEBRUARY 1980
City of Birth:	[redacted]
State/Province of Birth:	HIDALGO
Country/Region of Birth:	MEXICO - HIDALGO
Country/Region of Origin (Nationality):	MEXICO
Document Type:	PASSPORT
Document ID:	[redacted]
Country/Authority that Issued Document:	MEXICO
Issuance Date:	29 MAY 2015
Expiration Date:	29 MAY 2021
Do you hold or have you held any nationality other than the one you have indicated above?	NO
Present Address:	[redacted]
City:	TULACINGO
State/Province:	HIDALGO
Postal Zone/ZIP Code:	DOES NOT APPLY
Country/Region:	MEXICO
From Date:	JUNE 2005
Have you lived anywhere other than this address since the age of sixteen?	YES
Previous Address (1):	HOKUMAHOE ST.
City	LAUPAHOEHOE
State/Province:	HAWAII
Postal Zone/ZIP Code:	96764

Country/Region:	UNITED STATES OF AMERICA
From:	FEBRUARY 2004
To:	JUNE 2005
Previous Address (2):	LOC PARADONES S N BAR HUITZILINGO
City	
State/Province:	
Postal Zone/ZIP Code:	43730
Country/Region:	MEXICO
From:	MARCH 2003
To:	APRIL 2004
Previous Address (3):	HOKUMAHOE ST.
City	LAUPAHOEHOE
State/Province:	HAWAII
Postal Zone/ZIP Code:	96764
Country/Region:	UNITED STATES OF AMERICA
From:	APRIL 2001
To:	MARCH 2003
Previous Address (4):	LOC PAREDONES S N BARR HUITZILINGO
City	
State/Province:	
Postal Zone/ZIP Code:	43730
Country/Region:	MEXICO
From:	FEBRUARY 1996
To:	APRIL 2001
Primary Phone Number:	8082255279
Secondary Phone Number:	DOES NOT APPLY
Work Phone Number:	DOES NOT APPLY
Email Address:	
Is your Mailing Address the same as your Present Address?	NO
Mailing Address:	LISTA DE CORREOS
City:	
State/Province:	
Postal Zone/ZIP Code:	43600
Country/Region:	MEXICO
Permanent Address	
Name of person currently living at address:	
U.S. Address:	
Phone Number:	
Is this address where you want your Permanent Residence	YES

U.S. DEPARTMENT of STATE
CONSULAR ELECTRONIC APPLICATION CENTER

Online Immigrant Visa and Alien Registration Application (DS-260)

Family Information

Father's Surnames:	ROLDAN MARTINEZ
Father's Given Names:	
Date of Birth:	20 DECEMBER 1951
City of Birth:	
State/Province of Birth:	DO NOT KNOW
Country/Region of Birth:	MEXICO - HIDALGO
Is your father still living?	NO
Year of death:	1988
Mother's Surnames at Birth:	
Mother's Given Names:	
Date of Birth:	24 APRIL 1962
City of Birth:	
State/Province of Birth:	DO NOT KNOW
Country/Region of Birth:	MEXICO - HIDALGO
Is your mother still living?	YES
Current Address:	
City:	
State/Province:	
Postal Zone/ZIP Code:	43633
Country/Region:	MEXICO
Spouse's Full Name:	
Spouse's Date of Birth:	22 JANUARY 1976
Spouse's City of Birth:	HONOLULU
Spouse's State/Province of Birth:	HAWAII
Spouse's Country/Region of Birth:	UNITED STATES OF AMERICA
Spouse's Address:	SAME AS INTENDED U.S. ADDRESS
Occupation:	OTHER
Specify other:	FINANCIAL SERVICE REPRESENTATIVE
Date of Marriage:	28 JULY 2005
Marriage City:	
Marriage State/Province:	
Marriage Country/Region:	MEXICO
Is your spouse immigrating to the U.S.with you?	NO
Is your spouse immigrating to the U.S. at a later date to join you?	NO

Do you have any Previous Spouses?	NO
Do you have any children?	YES
Number of Children:	2
Child Name (1):	
Date of Birth:	01 MARCH 2005
City of Birth:	HILO
State of Birth:	HAWAII
Country/Region of Birth:	UNITED STATES OF AMERICA
Dose this child live with you?	NO
Address:	
City:	HONOLULU
State/Province:	HAWAII
Postal Zone/ZIP Code:	96819
Country/Region:	UNITED STATES OF AMERICA
Is this child immigrating to the U.S. with you?	NO
Is this child immigrating to the U.S. at a later date to join you?	NO
Child Name (2):	
Date of Birth:	09 OCTOBER 2012
City of Birth:	HONOLULU
State of Birth:	HAWAII
Country/Region of Birth:	UNITED STATES OF AMERICA
Dose this child live with you?	NO
Address:	
City:	HONOLULU
State/Province:	HAWAII
Postal Zone/ZIP Code:	96819
Country/Region:	UNITED STATES OF AMERICA
Is this child immigrating to the U.S. with you?	NO
Is this child immigrating to the U.S. at a later date to join you?	NO

U.S. DEPARTMENT of STATE
CONSULAR ELECTRONIC APPLICATION CENTER

Online Immigrant Visa and Alien Registration Application (DS-260)

Previous U.S. Travel Information

Have you ever been in the U.S.?	YES
Were you issued an Alien Registration Number by the Department of Homeland Security?	NO
Provide information on your last five U.S. visits.	
Date Arrived: (1) :	01 APRIL 2001
Length of Stay:	2 YEAR(S)
Date Arrived: (2) :	01 APRIL 2004
Length of Stay:	1 YEAR(S)
Have you ever been issued a U.S. Visa?	NO
Have you ever been refused a U.S. Visa, been refused admission to the United States, or withdrawn your application for admission at the port of entry?	YES
Explain:	IN 2004, I ENTERED EWI AND WAS RETURNED

U.S. DEPARTMENT of STATE
CONSULAR ELECTRONIC APPLICATION CENTER

Online Immigrant Visa and Alien Registration Application (DS-260)

Work / Education / Training Information

Primary Occupation:	OTHER
Specify Other:	CONSTRUCTION
Present Employer or School Name:	SELF EMPLOYED
Address:	209 CALLE CEDROS COL. VIVEROS DE LA LOMA
City:	TULANCINGO
State/Province:	HIDALGO
Postal Zone/ZIP Code:	DOES NOT APPLY
Country/Region:	MEXICO
Do you have other occupations?	NO
In which occupation do you intend to work in the U.S.?	OTHER
Specify Other:	CONSTRUCTION
Were you previously employed?	NO
Have you attended any educational institutions at a secondary level or above?	NO
Have you ever served in the military?	NO
Have you belonged to, contributed to, or worked for any professional, social, or charitable organization?	NO
Do you have any specialized skills or training, including firearms, explosives, nuclear, biological, or chemical experience?	NO
Have you ever served in, been a member of, or been involved with a paramilitary unit, vigilante unit, rebel group, guerrilla group, or insurgent organization?	NO
Can you speak and/or read languages other than your native language?	NO

U.S. DEPARTMENT of STATE
CONSULAR ELECTRONIC APPLICATION CENTER

Online Immigrant Visa and Alien Registration Application (DS-260)

Petitioner Information

Petitioner is my:	SPOUSE
Petitioner Name:	
Petitioner Address:	
City:	HONOLULU
State/Province:	HAWAII
Postal Zone/ZIP Code:	96819
Country/Region:	UNITED STATES OF AMERICA
Telephone:	
Mobile/Cell Telephone:	
Email Address:	

U.S. DEPARTMENT of STATE
CONSULAR ELECTRONIC APPLICATION CENTER

Online Immigrant Visa and Alien Registration Application (DS-260)

Security and Background Information

Do you have a communicable disease of public health significance such as tuberculosis (TB)?	NO
Do you have documentation to establish that you have received vaccinations in accordance with U.S. law?	YES
Do you have a mental or physical disorder that poses or is likely to pose a threat to the safety or welfare of yourself or others?	NO
Are you or have you ever been a drug abuser or addict?	NO
Have you ever been arrested or convicted for any offense or crime, even though subject of a pardon, amnesty, or other similar action?	NO
Have you ever violated, or engaged in a conspiracy to violate, any law relating to controlled substances?	NO
Are you the spouse, son, or daughter of an individual who has violated any controlled substance trafficking law, and have knowingly benefited from the trafficking activities in the past five years?	NO
Are you coming to the United States to engage in prostitution or unlawful commercialized vice or have you been engaged in prostitution or procuring prostitutes within the past 10 years?	NO
Have you ever been involved in, or do you seek to engage in, money laundering?	NO
Have you ever committed or conspired to commit a human trafficking offense in the United States or outside the United States?	NO
Have you ever knowingly aided, abetted, assisted, or colluded with an individual who has been identified by the President of the United States as a person who plays a significant role in a severe form of trafficking in persons?	NO
Are you the spouse, son, or daughter of an individual who has committed or conspired to commit a human trafficking offense in the United States or outside the United States and have you within the last five years, knowingly benefited from the trafficking activities?	NO
Do you seek to engage in espionage, sabotage, export control violations, or any other illegal activity while in the United States?	NO
Do you seek to engage in terrorist activities while in the United States or have you ever engaged in terrorist activities?	NO
Have you ever or do you intend to provide financial assistance or other support to terrorists or terrorist organizations?	NO
Are you a member or representative of a terrorist organization?	NO
Have you ever ordered, incited, committed, assisted, or otherwise participated in genocide?	NO
Have you ever committed, ordered, incited, assisted, or otherwise participated in torture?	NO
Have you committed, ordered, incited, assisted, or otherwise participated in extrajudicial killings, political killings, or other acts of violence?	NO
Have you ever engaged in the recruitment of or the use of child soldiers?	NO
Have you, while serving as a government official, been responsible for or directly carried out, at any time, particularly severe violations of religious freedom?	NO
Are you a member of or affiliated with the Communist or other totalitarian party?	NO
Have you ever directly or indirectly assisted or supported any of the groups in Columbia known as the Revolutionary Armed Forces of Columbia (FARC), National Liberation Army (ELN), or United Self-Defense Forces of Columbia (AUC)?	NO
Have you ever, through abuse of governmental or political position converted for personal gain, confiscated or expropriated property in a foreign nation to which a United States national had claim of	NO

Are you the spouse, minor child, or agent of an individual who has through abuse of governmental or political position converted for personal gain, confiscated or expropriated property in a foreign nation to which a United States national had claim of ownership?	NO
Have you ever been directly involved in the establishment or enforcement of population controls forcing a woman to undergo an abortion against her free choice or a man or a woman to undergo sterilization against his or her free choice?	NO
Have you ever disclosed or trafficked in confidential U.S. business information obtained in connection with U.S. participation in the Chemical Weapons Convention?	NO
Are you the spouse, minor child, or agent of an individual who has disclosed or trafficked in confidential U.S. business information obtained in connection with U.S. participation in the Chemical Weapons Convention?	NO
Have you ever sought to obtain or assist others to obtain a visa, entry into the United States, or any other United States immigration benefit by fraud or willful misrepresentation or other unlawful means?	YES
Explain: IN 2004, I CROSSED THE BORDER IN ARIZONA UNDOCUMENTED BUT WAS CAUGHT BY US BORDER PATROL. THIS ILLEGAL CROSSING WAS DOCUMENTED AND THE US IMMIGRATION HAS A RECORD OF IT.	
Have you ever been the subject of a removal or deportation hearing?	NO
Have you failed to attend a hearing on removability or inadmissibility within the last five years?	NO
Have you ever been unlawfully present, overstayed the amount of time granted by an immigration official or otherwise violated the terms of a U.S. visa?	NO
Are you subject to a civil penalty under INA 274C?	NO
Have you been ordered removed from the U.S. during the last five years?	NO
Have you been ordered removed from the U.S. for a second time within the last 20 years?	NO
Have you ever been unlawfully present and ordered removed from the U.S. during the last ten years?	NO
Have you ever been convicted of an aggravated felony and been ordered removed from the U.S.?	NO
Have you ever been unlawfully present in the U.S. for more than 180 days (but no more than one year) and have voluntarily departed the U.S. within the last three years?	NO
Have you ever been unlawfully present in the U.S. for more than one year or more than one year in the aggregate at any time during the last 10 years?	NO
Have you ever withheld custody of a U.S. citizen child outside the United States from a person granted legal custody by a U.S. court?	NO
Have you ever intentionally assisted another person in withholding custody of a U.S. citizen child outside the United States from a person granted legal custody by a U.S. court?	NO
Have you voted in the United States in violation of any law or regulation?	NO
Have you ever renounced United States citizenship for the purpose of avoiding taxation?	NO
Have you attended a public elementary school or a public secondary school on student (F) status after November 30, 1996 without reimbursing the school?	NO
Do you seek to enter the United States for the purpose of performing skilled or unskilled labor but have not yet been certified by the Secretary of Labor?	NO
Are you a graduate of a foreign medical school seeking to perform medical services in the United States but have not yet passed the National Board of Medical Examiners examination or its equivalent?	NO
Are you a health care worker seeking to perform such work in the United States but have not yet received certification from the Commission on Graduates of Foreign Nursing Schools or from an equivalent approved independent credentialing organization?	NO
Are you permanently ineligible for U.S. citizenship?	NO
Have you ever departed the United States in order to evade military service during a time of war?	NO
Are you coming to the U.S. to practice polygamy?	NO
Are you a former exchange visitor (J) who has not yet fulfilled the two-year foreign residence requirement?	NO
Has the Secretary of Homeland Security of the United States ever determined that you knowingly made a frivolous application for asylum?	NO

U.S. DEPARTMENT of STATE
CONSULAR ELECTRONIC APPLICATION CENTER

Online Immigrant Visa and Alien Registration Application (DS-260)

Social Security Number Information

Have you ever applied for a Social Security number?	NO
Do you want the Social Security Administration to issue a Social Security number and a card?	YES
Do you authorize disclosure of information from this form to the Department of Homeland Security, the Social Security Administration, and such other U.S. Government agencies as may be required for the purposes of assigning you a social security number (SSN) and issuing you a Social Security card and do you authorize the Social Security Administration to share your SSN with the Department of Homeland Security?	YES

U.S. DEPARTMENT of STATE
CONSULAR ELECTRONIC APPLICATION CENTER

Online Immigrant Visa and Alien Registration Application (DS-260)

Social Security Number Information

Have you ever applied for a Social Security number?	NO
Do you want the Social Security Administration to issue a Social Security number and a card?	YES
Do you authorize disclosure of information from this form to the Department of Homeland Security, the Social Security Administration, and such other U.S. Government agencies as may be required for the purposes of assigning you a social security number (SSN) and issuing you a Social Security card and do you authorize the Social Security Administration to share your SSN with the Department of Homeland Security?	YES

U.S. DEPARTMENT of STATE
CONSULAR ELECTRONIC APPLICATION CENTER

Online Immigrant Visa and Alien Registration Application (DS-260)

Immigrant Visa and Alien Registration Application Confirmation

Thank You

Your Immigrant Visa and Alien Registration Application form (Form DS-260) has been automatically forwarded to your interview location.

This confirms the submission of the Immigrant Visa and Alien Registration application for:

Name Provided:	
Country/Region of Origin (Nationality):	MEXICO
Completed On:	14 AUG 2017
Case No:	CDJ2016801007
Confirmation No:	AA006ZINV8

C D J 2 0 1 6 8 0 1 0 0 7

A A 0 0 6 Z I N V 8

THIS IS NOT A VISA

Version 01.01.00

ABOUT THE AUTHOR

Brian D. Lerner is an Immigration Lawyer and runs a National Immigration Law Firm for nearly 30 years. He is an attorney who is a certified specialist that might help in Immigration & Nationality Law as issued by the California State Bar, Board of Legal Specialization. Attorney Lerner is an expert in Immigration Law, Removal and Deportation, Citizenship, Waiver and Appeals.

He has been a licensed attorney since 1992 and started the Law Offices of Brian D. Lerner, APC. The immigration practice consists of Immigration and Nationality Law, and everything involved with and regarding immigration which includes citizenship, investment visas, family and employment visas, removal and deportation hearings, appeals, waivers, adjustment, consulate processing and all types of immigration and citizenship matters.

He has represented clients from all over the U.S. and in many countries around the world. One side of his practice is dedicated to keeping people in the U.S. and fighting for their immigration rights, while another side is to get people back who have been deported and removed from the U.S.

Also, there is the affirmative part of Immigration Law which Brian Lerner has helped numerous people come into the U.S. on business visas, investment visas, student visas, fiancée and marriage visas, religious visas and many more. Attorney Lerner has helped immigrants who are victims of crime and domestic violence or ones that are married to abusers.

In other words, Attorney Lerner has a firm that helps people all over the U.S. He has dedicated significant time to preparing numerous petitions and applications for you to get at a fraction of the price of hiring an attorney. He says it is the next best thing to a real attorney because they are real petitions prepared by an expert.

www.ingramcontent.com/pod-product-compliance
Lightning Source LLC
LaVergne TN
LVHW060041210926
848481LV00013B/3926

9781958990445